BU
STA

ebuilding®

The Taunton Press

Inspiration for hands-on living®

The Taunton Press, Inc., 63 South Main Street, PO Box 5506, Newtown, CT 06470-5506

e-mail: tp@taunton.com

Jacket/Cover design: Cathy Cassidy

Interior design: Cathy Cassidy

Layout: Carol Petro

Front Cover Photographer: Andy Engel, courtesy *Fine Homebuilding,* © The Taunton Press, Inc.

Back Cover Photographers: (clockwise from top left) Charles Bickford, courtesy *Fine Homebuilding,* © The Taunton Press, Inc.; Charles Miller, courtesy *Fine Homebuilding,* © The Taunton Press, Inc.; Charles Bickford, courtesy *Fine Homebuilding,* © The Taunton Press, Inc.; Scott Phillips, courtesy *Fine Homebuilding,* © The Taunton Press, Inc.

Taunton's For Pros By Pros® and Fine Homebuilding® are trademarks of The Taunton Press, Inc., registered in the U.S. Patent and Trademark Office.

Library of Congress Cataloging-in-Publication Data

Building stairs / from the editors of Fine homebuilding.

   p. cm. -- (For pros, by pros)

Includes index.

  ISBN-13: 978-1-56158-653-0

  ISBN-10: 1-56158-653-6

  1. Stair building. I. Fine homebuilding. II. Series.

TH5667.B86 2004

694'.6--dc22

                    2003020650

Printed in the United States of America

10 9 8 7

The following manufacturers/names appearing in *Building Stairs* are trademarks:

Bondo®, Calculated Industries®, ChemRex®, Inc., Disney®, Dremel®, Dura Seal®, Hitachi® #C15FB, Hot Stuff Super T®, Porter-Cable®, Scale Master®, Simpson®, Skil®, Thompson Minwax®, Tightbond® ES747, Titebond® II, Titebond® Supreme, Ulmia®, Watco®, Weldwood®

Special thanks to the authors, editors, art directors,
copy editors, and other staff members of *Fine Homebuilding*
who contributed to the development of the articles in this book.

CONTENTS

█ PART 3: CURVED STAIRWAYS

█ PART 4: SPECIAL STAIRWAYS

INTRODUCTION

Like gunslingers sizing each other up in a Hollywood Western, newly acquainted carpenters always want to know how good the other is. Inevitably, one poses the defining question: "Can you build stairs?"

The original meaning of the word "masterpiece" was work that a journeyman executed to prove that he had mastered his craft. For a house carpenter, no project combines the range of skills that stair building does. Even in a simple house, a staircase is a complex thing. You have to calculate the size and number of steps carefully. You have to choose stout material for the structural members and cut them precisely. Then you have to bring a furniture maker's fussiness to the trim work because, in many homes, stairs are not just a practical means of getting from one floor to the other—they are also an architectural centerpiece.

Fortunately for all of us, you don't have to be a master carpenter to build a good staircase. But you do need to know what you're doing, which is where this book comes in. Collected here are 21 articles from *Fine Homebuilding* magazine. Written by experienced builders from all over the country, these articles cover everything from simple basement steps to exotic curved stairways.

A word of caution: The building codes that govern stairs are changing all the time, so not all of the projects featured here comply with current national codes. If you're building any staircase, be sure to check with your local building department. And remember, as Tracy Kidder wrote in his book *House*, "Stair-making carpenters are like school crossing guards or trainers of seeing-eye dogs. They take on one of society's small sacred trusts."

—Kevin Ireton,
editor-in-chief, *Fine Homebuilding*

Cutting Out Basic Stairs

BY ERIC PFAFF

started out as a laborer on a framing crew ten years ago. After a few months I began feeling cocky about my framing skills and one day decided that I was going to impress the boss. I asked him if I could cut a simple set of basement stairs while he was on lunch break. He told me to go for it, though he wasn't going to pay me extra for working through lunch. Anxious to prove myself, I agreed to his terms.

I worked frantically, first figuring the rise and run, then cutting the stringers as fast as I could. I was just nailing the last of the treads when the boss came back from lunch. He seemed surprised that I had gotten the steps done, but the real surprise came when he smacked his forehead on the stairwell header. In my haste I had miscalculated the headroom over the stairs and never got a raise while working with that crew.

Measure the Height of the Stairs Where They Land on the Floor

I've cut over 100 sets of steps since I gave my boss that concussion, and I now realize that the first and most important step in stair building is accurately calculating the rise, or the height of each step, and the run, or the width of each step. I begin by finding the overall rise, or the distance between the two floors that the stairs will connect.

In a perfect world all floors would be flat and level, and measuring the rise would mean simply running a tape from the floor above to the floor below. However, I've seen floors—especially in basements—that slope a couple of inches from one wall to the other.

The first and most important step in stair building is accurately calculating the rise, or the height of each step, and the run, or the width of each step.

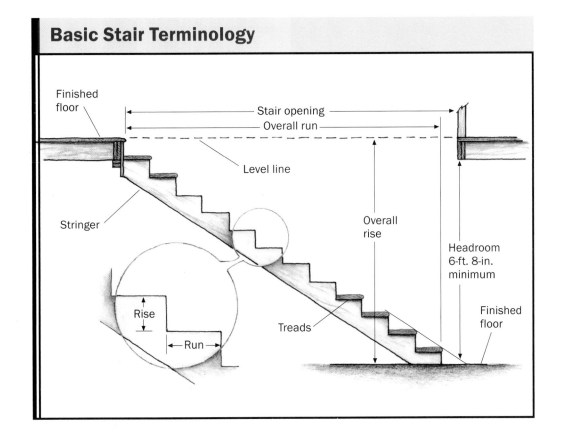

Basic Stair Terminology

Finished floor

Stair opening

Overall run

Level line

Stringer

Overall rise

Headroom 6-ft. 8-in. minimum

Rise

Run

Treads

Finished floor

The way around this problem is measuring the overall rise as close as possible to where the stairs will land on the floor. I make this measurement by taping my 4-ft. level to a straight 2x4 that is at least as long as the framed opening for the stair (photo below). Keeping the 2x4 level, I measure up to it near to where I figure the stairs will land. In the stair featured here, the overall rise is 99½ in.

Measuring the overall rise. A 2x4 extends a 4-ft. level over to where the staircase will land. Measuring the rise at this point minimizes the chance of error from a basement floor that might not be level.

Figuring Rise and Run

Many codebooks and safety officials insist that all stairs have a 7-in. rise and an 11-in. run. However, the formulas below are also routinely used to determine rise and run.

1. The rise times the run should equal approximately 75 in.
2. Two times the rise plus one run should equal 25 in.
3. Rise plus run should be 17 in.–18 in.

Check Local Codes before Cutting Your Stairs

Before I explain my calculations, let me say a brief word about stairs and the codebook. Code requirements for stairs seem to change with every new codebook and can vary greatly from state to state, sometimes even from town to town. For instance, some codes require a 7-in. maximum rise; others allow an 8-in. rise. So check with your local building inspector to make sure that any stairs you build meet the local code. For the project featured here, I was replacing an existing set of basement stairs. My floor heights were fixed, as was the rough opening in the floor, so I had to work within the constraints of the existing framing. Consequently, these stairs are steeper than most codes allow. But the building code in use at the time they were built allowed exceptions when replacing existing stairways.

Generally, I think a 7½-in. rise with a 10-in. run produces a safe, comfortable stair, so as a starting point, I divided my overall rise by 7.5, which gave me 13.266 rises. You can't have a partial step, so I divided the total rise by the nearest whole number, in this case 13. The result is 7.653, or very close to 7¹¹⁄₁₆ in. for each individual rise.

Now that I know how many steps I'll have, I can figure out the depth, or run, of each tread. The header that will support the staircase at the top of the stairs will act as the first riser, so the stringers actually end up with 12 risers and 12 treads. (In every stair, you'll have one less tread than the number of risers.) For maximum headroom I'd like the bottom step to land directly below the other end of the framed opening, which is 108 in. long. So I divide 108 in. by 12, the number of treads, and end up with a tread depth of 9 in. As mentioned previously, code requirements for stairs may vary, as well as the formulas for calculating safe and comfortable stairs (see the sidebar at left). My local building officials tell me that the rise plus the run of a stairway should be 17 in. to 18 in. At 16¹¹⁄₁₆ in., this staircase is a bit steeper than I'd like. Again, I'm restricted by the existing framing, but I'd rather have a slightly steep stair than compromise the headroom clearance. For this project, the inspector agreed with me.

Stair Gauges Help with the Stringer Layout

A stringer, or carriage, is the diagonal framing member that holds the treads (and the risers, if they're used). I like to use straight, kiln-dried Douglas fir 2x12s for stringers whenever possible. I start by setting a 2x12 on sawhorses with the crown, if any, facing toward me. A framing square is the best tool for laying out the sawtooth pattern of treads and risers on the stringer. But I also use stair gauges, which screw onto the framing square and increase the speed and accuracy of the layout (see the top photo at right). Available at most hardware stores, these little beauties are small hexagonal blocks of aluminum or brass with a slot cut in them so that they slip over a framing square. Thumb screws or knurled nuts hold them in place on the square. I put one gauge at the rise number on the short side of the square (the tongue) and the other at the run on the long side of the square (the blade). The gauges register against the edge of the 2x12 and keep the square orientation on the stringer consistent for every step.

The Thickness of a Tread Is Subtracted from the Bottom of the Stringer

As I move down the stringer and lay out the steps, I line up the edge of my rise with the run line from the step above. I repeat the process all the way down the stringer until I have the right number of rises, in this case 12.

Stair gauges streamline layout. Small clips called stair gauges are attached to the framing square at rise and run measurements to keep the orientation of the framing square the same for each step layout.

Subtract the thickness of a tread. For the bottom rise to be the correct height, the thickness of one tread must be subtracted from the bottom of the stringer. Moving the square to the other side of the stringer makes it easier to complete the lines.

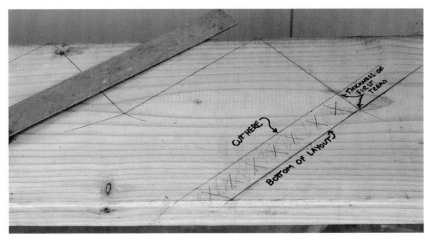

Label lines to avoid confusion when cutting the board.

After I've drawn the last rise on the bottom of the stringer, I square it back using my framing square (see the middle photo on p. 7). If the stringers were cut and installed and the treads put on at this point, the bottom step would be higher than the rest of the steps by the thickness of the tread. I solve this problem by subtracting that thickness from the bottom of the stringer, which lowers the stringer assembly. That way, when the stair treads are installed, all of the rises will be the same.

As a word of caution, the overall rise of the stair should be calculated from the finished floor above to the finished floor below. If you didn't compensate in your original measurement, adding finished flooring after stairs are built will result in a top or a bottom step different from the rest, which creates a dangerous stair.

Because my treads will be made out of 2x10s, I measure up 1½ in. from the bottom of the stringer. I always label my lines to avoid confusion when cutting (see the bottom photo on p. 7).

Overcutting Can Weaken the Stringer

After laying out the stringer, it's time for me to cut the rises and the runs. I make my initial cuts with a circular saw, making careful, steady cuts for all of the rise and run lines along the length of the stringer. I take care not to overcut the lines, which would substantially weaken the stringer. Instead, I finish my rise and run cuts with a jigsaw (see the bottom photo at right).

After the stringer is cut, I set it in place temporarily to make sure that it fits and that it's level. I figure out exactly where the stringer will rest against the header of the stair opening by measuring down from the floor the distance of the rise plus the thickness of the tread ($7\frac{11}{16} + 1\frac{1}{2} = 9\frac{3}{16}$ in.). I make a level line across the header at this mea-

First cuts are made with a circular saw. Overcutting the lines will weaken the stringer, so the initial cuts with a circular saw should never extend beyond the layout lines.

Finishing the cut. A jigsaw is used to complete the cuts in each corner, cutting the wood that the circular saw can't get. A handsaw will also work instead of a jigsaw.

surement and tack my stringer in place so that the top of the stringer is even with this line. For this stairway I had to extend the header down with a 2x4 and plywood to give me more to attach the stringer to.

Next I test several of the steps with a torpedo level. Once I'm satisfied with the stringer, I take it down and use it as a template to lay out and cut the second stringer (see the top photo on the facing page). I make sure that the sawtooth points on the template stringer point in the same direction as the crown of the second 2x12.

The second stringer is cut the same as the first, and then both stringers are tacked in place and checked for level. This time I check the runs on the individual stringers

The first stringer becomes a template. Once the first stringer has been cut and tested in place, it can be traced for the layout of the second stringer. The crown of the stringer stock must be facing the same direction as the points on the template.

Not only are railings an essential part of stair safety, they are also the law.

for level and also use my 4-ft. level to make sure they are level with each other (see the photo at right). If a staircase with 1½-in.-thick treads is more than 36 in. wide, it's necessary to use three stringers. Again, it's best to check with your local building official if you have any doubts or questions.

Strongbacks Take the Flex out of the Stringers

Before I install the stringers permanently, I add strongbacks to each one (see the top photo on p. 10). Strongbacks are 2x4s nailed at right angles to the stringer and run their entire length. I nail the strongbacks through the stringers with 16d nails every 8 in. Putting them on the outside of the stringers lets the stringers be closer together, which reduces the span of the treads and makes the stairs feel more stiff. Strongbacks stiffen the stringer by limiting lateral flex.

After the strongbacks are nailed on, I install the stringers for good. I nail them securely at the top through the plywood

Both stringers are tested together. Before the stringers can be installed, both are set up and leveled individually. A 4-ft. level then tests them in relation to one another.

Strongbacks stiffen the stringers. Strongbacks, or 2x4 stiffeners, are nailed to the sides of the stringers to keep them from flexing.

Treads are attached with screws. Screwing the treads to the stringers is the best way to keep the staircase from squeaking. Predrilling the holes prevents the screws from snapping while they're being driven.

header extension from behind and into a 2x4 spacer block between the stringers. At the bottom a length of pressure-treated 2x nailed to the concrete with powder-actuated fasteners serves as a nailer as well as a spacer between the bottom ends of the stringers. Some builders like to notch the bottom of the stringers around the nailer. But with the bottom step already cut 1½ in. narrower for the thickness of the tread, notching out for the nailer leaves a thin and precarious section of diagonal grain that is more likely to split when the treads are attached or to break off if I trip over the stringer before the treads are installed.

The final step is putting on the treads. I cut the treads for this stairway out of 2x10s and attach them to the stringers with 3-in. screws. Screws are the best way to keep the treads from squeaking, and if there is ever a problem, they can be removed quickly without damaging either the tread or the stringer. I predrill my holes, especially if I'm using bugle-headed construction screws, which can snap as they're going in.

One important item that I'm obviously leaving out is the railing system. Not only are railings an essential part of stair safety, they are also the law. This stairway will be enclosed with a wall on the open side, and handrails will be hung on each wall to make the stairway complete. Stair railings are a topic for another article.

Eric Pfaff is founder and principal of Architectural Automations, *which automates multi-sliding doors. He is the author of* The Quicky Stair Book.

A Site-Built Stair

■ BY ALEXANDER BRENNEN

It's easy to see why carpenters are attracted to stairs. Along with framing a roof, building a staircase is one of the most challenging geometrical tasks in building a house. And once the variables of rise, run, headroom, railing, and landing configurations have been resolved, the carpenter assigned to build the stair can look forward to airing out some of the finish-carpentry tools that have been languishing in the corners of his toolbox.

Architects can also fall victim to the spell of a well-turned stair, and they often design elaborate stairs—no doubt at the request of their clients. Unfortunately, complicated stairs are frequently beyond the budget. Sometimes they must even be built off site and reassembled in place. A pleasing staircase can, however, be built using standard on-site carpentry methods. This article is about such a stair. It connects the ground floor of a turn-of-the-century Arts and Crafts-style house to a new upstairs addition, designed by architect Glen Jarvis.

From the ground floor up, the stair has two primary flights connected by a landing. Another landing on the second floor leads to a short flight with only three risers. Glen's original design for the stair detailed a traditional oak balustrade assembled from manu-

Rising from what once was a bedroom, this new stair leads to a second-story addition on a turn-of-the-century Arts and Crafts home. Builder Alexander Brennen built the stair on site, using Douglas fir newel posts, and oak treads and risers to match the flooring; railings and balusters to correspond with the original trim elements.

factured parts. But as we got further into calculating the costs of the remodel, it became clear that the money wasn't going to be available for expensive stair parts and their fastidious fitting. Jarvis and I met with the owners of the house, Morris and Regina Beatus, mulled over our options, and decided to build a simpler stair in keeping with the original house. The treads and risers would still be oak, for its durability and to match the oak floor in the upper and lower halls. The railing would be of clear Douglas fir, which would match the door and window trim.

Horses on Rake Walls

Once we had the second floor framed and the roof in place, we calculated the rise of the stair by measuring the distance from the existing oak strip floor in the lower hall to the top of the subfloor in the upper hall. To this number we added ⁵⁄₁₆ in. to account for the thickness of the oak strip flooring that would cover the upper-hall floor. We then divided this number by the number of risers to establish the riser height. For this stair, the rise ended up at 7¾ in. and the run at 10 in.

The landing between the two primary flights of stairs is 6 ft. wide, which is the minimum width allowable by our code to accommodate our 3-ft.-wide treads—also a code minimum. Once we knew our riser heights, we began our stair framing by building the lower landing first. There was nothing tricky about this part of the project because we used standard framing lumber and conventional stud-wall construction techniques to build the stair's superstructure (see the photo below). The stair horses (also called carriages, stair stringers, or stair jacks in some parts of the country) were cut from 2x12s. On the open side they bear on 2x4 rake walls. On the wall side they are affixed with 16d nails to ledgers that are anchored to the stud walls (see the drawing on p. 16). Drywall backing blocks made from 2x10 stock fill the stud bays adjacent to the 2x6 ledgers. Once we had the landings and horses in place, we installed some temporary treads and didn't work further on the stair until the drywall work was complete.

Newel Posts and Treads

The newel posts are 4x4s made of clear, dry Douglas fir. I notched the bottoms of each post to fit beside the stair horse (see the drawing on the facing page) or the landing rim joists. After plumbing each newel post so that it was parallel with the rise of the stair, I glued each one to the framing with PL 400 subfloor adhesive from ChemRex®, Inc. and secured each with a pair of ⅜-in. machine bolts. In places where I couldn't run the bolts, I used a half dozen 4-in. galvanized drywall screws driven from different angles to lock the post firmly in place.

I had planned to use the laminated oak-tread stock available from our regular supplier, but after learning that I could buy enough 4/4 red oak to make the treads, risers, and skirtboards (sometimes called stringboards) for the same amount of money it would cost to buy just the premade treads, I decided to make my own. To trim the treads, I would use 1¹⁄₁₆-in.-sq. bullnose trim

Two straight flights of stairs engage the first landing, which is built using standard stud-wall framing techniques and materials.

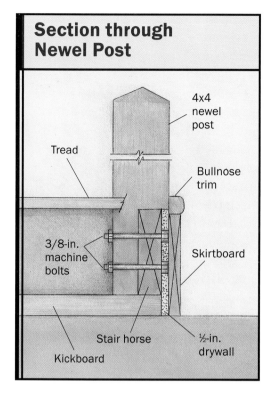

Section through Newel Post

4x4 newel post

Tread

Bullnose trim

3/8-in. machine bolts

Skirtboard

Stair horse

Kickboard

½-in. drywall

ter a couple of passes to put their faces in plane, I ended up with pieces ¾ in. thick. I then jointed their edges and ripped all the various parts to size on the table saw.

Job-Site Assembly

Once the drywall crew was through making and cleaning up their traditional mess, I brought all my oak stair parts to the site. At last I could yank the temporary treads off the stair horses and get down to business. I installed the skirtboards first. On the wall side they tucked against the drywall in the gap between the horses and the 2x6 ledger. After cutting the outside skirtboards to fit at

Risers and skirtboards are cross-nailed and glued where they meet at mitered corners. Here, a tread notched to accommodate a landing newel post is lowered onto a fresh line of aliphatic resin glue.

A sharp block plane is a necessity on a job like this— I kept mine busy on every phase of the finish work.

on the front and open side. Using a separate piece for the bullnose trim would allow me to wrap the treads around the newel posts easily and to hide the end grain of the treads.

In our area, the most economical red oak is available from a local supplier who has a pile of it in random widths and random lengths. The boards are planed on two sides and jointed on one edge only. In any given stack, most pieces are from 4 in. to 6 in. wide and about 8 ft. long. I found a few wide pieces in the pile that could be used for skirtboards and risers. Then I picked out boards that were wide enough to allow me to rip them into 5-in. boards.

Working in my shop, I cut the boards in half and glued their edges together to make 10-in.-wide, 4-ft.-long planks. This would be the tread stock. Because the planks were cut from the same board, their grain matched well and their figure had more character than the premade treads, which are often glued up from 2-in.-wide pieces.

After gluing up the treads I ran all the oak through a 12-in. thickness planer/jointer. Af-

After beveling the tops of the posts with a saw, Brennen dresses the cuts with a sharp block plane.

Sources

ChemRex, Inc.
889 Valley Park Dr.
Shakopee, MN 55379
(800) 433-9517
www.chemrex.com

W. L. Fuller, Inc.
P.O. Box 8767
7 Cypress St.
Warwick, RI 02888
(401) 467-2900
www.wlfuller.com

top and bottom, I clamped them in place and marked them for the tread and riser cuts. The risers and outside skirtboards met at a 45° miter (see the top photo on p.13), so the layout mark represented the backside of the cut.

Because there are two outside skirtboards running in opposite directions, I needed to make miter cuts from opposite sides of the boards. Fortunately, my worm-drive Skil® saw tilts one way, while my Porter-Cable® worm-drive trim saw tilts the other way. I used sharp combination blades to make the cuts, and clamped straightedges to the skirtboards to guide them.

The skirtboards are affixed to the framing with 2-in. galvanized drywall screws. All the screw holes are plugged. To bore each screw hole and plug hole at the same time, I used a tool with a 6-in.-long ⅛-in.-dia. bit and a movable #6 countersink, which carves a ⅜-in.-dia. hole for a plug from W.L. Fuller.

I installed the treads and risers from the bottom up, fitting the first two risers and then the first tread. Each one had to be scribed to the skirtboard, and that's where having 4-ft. stock for 3-ft. treads came in handy. I could afford to be finicky about the fit, knowing I had some extra stock to let me whittle away at one end if need be. I marked my scribe lines with a sharp utility knife, and cut to the line with a trim saw set at a 2° bevel to give me a slight back-cut. Then I used a block plane to make minute adjustments. A sharp block plane is a necessity on a job like this—I kept mine busy on every phase of the finish work.

Alternating riser, then tread as I worked my way up the stair, I fastened the risers to the outer skirtboards and the treads to the horses with 8d galvanized finish nails and aliphatic resin glue. From the back of each riser I drove 2-in. galvanized drywall screws, 9 in. o. c., into predrilled holes in the adjacent treads, and used the same screws to anchor the leading edges of the treads to the risers below. They too are glued. I anchored the back edge of the top tread to a ledger

that is screwed and glued to the framing. Where a riser abuted a newel post, I checked to make sure that the post was plumb in both directions. If it wasn't, I leaned on the post a little, and drove screws through the riser into the post to bring it plumb. Once I had all the treads and risers in place, I glued and nailed bullnose trim to all the treads and around both landings.

I plugged the countersunk screw holes with oak plugs, and pared them flush with a chisel. Then I used a hand scraper to remove the excess glue and smooth out the edges between the treads and the bullnose trim. Using a scraper sounds fancy, but once you get the hang of sharpening it, the scraper is a very fast tool—especially when working with oak. Before bringing on the flooring subcontractor, I filled all the nail holes and sanded the entire stair.

Railing

I returned to the project to work on the railing and balusters after the two landings and

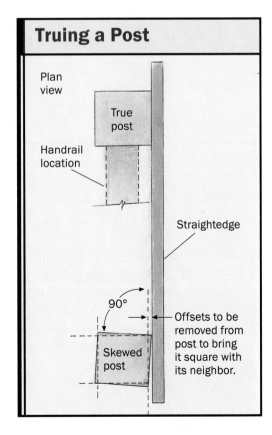

Truing a Post

Plan view

True post

Handrail location

Straightedge

90°

Skewed post

Offsets to be removed from post to bring it square with its neighbor.

the upstairs hall had been laid with oak strip flooring, and everything—stair included—had been finished with a light stain and three coats of polyurethane.

Simplicity remained our watchword, as we decided to use a stock mushroom-type handrail affixed to the top of a 2-in. by 2½-in. piece of Douglas fir (see the top photo at right) to give the railing some mass. But before I could install the railing between the posts, I needed to cut their tops to length.

I used my worm-drive saw along with a clamped-on guide to bevel the tops of the posts to a shallow peak (see the bottom photo at right). For this bevel, I set the base of the saw to make a 22.5° cut.

Next I used a long straightedge, held against adjacent posts, to see if they were square to one another. Nope. As shown in the drawing on the facing page, which is exaggerated for clarity, the posts were skewed in relation to one another. This didn't make any difference structurally, but it made it difficult to fit a railing precisely between them. To correct the situation, I marked the top of the skewed post and used my block plane (what else) to taper the post so as to put it in plane with its mate. Then I squared off this line to make each face of the post match its neighbor. This doctoring doesn't extend all the way down the post. It's actually a slight corkscrew that isn't noticeable.

I installed the lower portion of the railing first. I clamped it to both posts at the correct height (34 in. in this case) and used my knife to scribe the angle of cut directly on the rail. I made these cuts with a 14-in. power miter box, and left the setting the same for the handrail cuts. The lower portion of the rails I anchored to the newel posts with a couple of 3-in. galvanized drywall screws at each intersection. The screw holes were covered by the mushroom-cap portion of the railing, which I affixed to the bottom rail with glue and screws driven from below so that no fastener holes show on the topside of the rail.

The 2x2 balusters are spaced evenly on 5-in. centers. Two balusters fall on each tread, and they are toenailed to the treads from

To avoid splitting the ends of the balusters, Brennen predrills all nail holes while holding the piece in place.

Precise bevels. Using a clamped-on jig to guide his worm-drive saw, the author begins the first of four bevel cuts that will result in shallow, pyramidal tops for the newel posts. The cuts here were made with the saw set at 22.5°

opposite directions and to the underside of the handrail with 6d finish nails driven into predrilled holes. I laid out their positions on the treads and railing with light pencil marks, and cut all the balusters at once. There are two lengths, and I cut each one slightly long (1⁄64 in.) to allow myself some adjustment. After a test fit, I nailed each one in place, securing their tops first because the angle of the rail held them steady.

By the time I tacked the last baluster in place, Morris Beatus was ready to take over. He filled the nail holes, sanded the unfinished surfaces and then finished them with three coats of Watco® oil.

Alexander Brennen has been doing construction and cabinetmaking for 27 years. He lives in Berkley, CA.

Stair Assembly

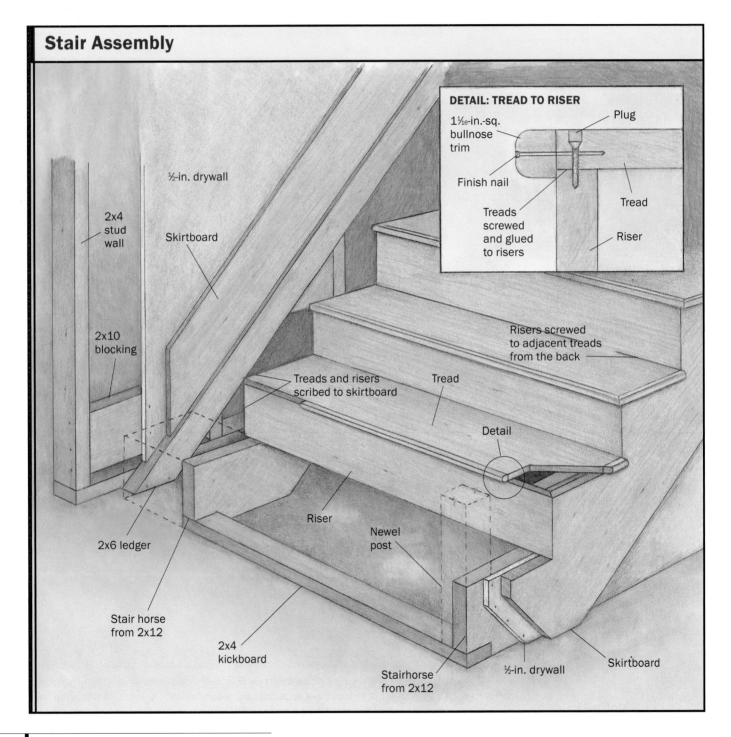

DETAIL: TREAD TO RISER

1 1⁄16-in.-sq. bullnose trim

Plug

Finish nail

Treads screwed and glued to risers

Tread

Riser

½-in. drywall

2x4 stud wall

Skirtboard

2x10 blocking

Treads and risers scribed to skirtboard

Tread

Risers screwed to adjacent treads from the back

Detail

2x6 ledger

Riser

Newel post

Stair horse from 2x12

2x4 kickboard

Stairhorse from 2x12

½-in. drywall

Skirtboard

Using a Story Pole to Lay Out Stairs

■ BY LON SCHLEINING

Imagine walking down a staircase with your arms full of Christmas packages. You seem to find each step without looking. At the landing, however, your foot reaches out to feel a surface that isn't there. The floor is not the height you think it should be and down you go, packages and all. Ask any personal-injury attorney if this story is familiar.

When you're framing stairs, the common practice is to do a quick layout on the stringers with a framing square, assume equal risers, and start sawing away. Nowhere in the framing of a house is the possibility for accumulated error greater than in framing stairs. If each rise is off just 1/16 in. (roughly the thickness of a pencil line), the accumulated error could be as much as an inch on a typical staircase.

Everything may seem fine until the job nears its end and the finish-floor coverings are installed. Suddenly, the first or last step is either too high or too low. The framing crew probably built the rough stair without taking into account the varying thickness of finish-floor materials, but by this time, the deed is done. Moreover, the solution to the problem usually involves more than adding a shim or two. All the resulting hair-pulling and finger-pointing could have been avoided if the framers had asked the right questions and had used a simple story pole.

A story pole can be a big help to anyone who frames staircases. Flooring, treads, and landings of varying thicknesses, as well as accumulated errors, all conspire against a plumb, level staircase with evenly spaced treads. After spending about 15 minutes to lay out the story pole for a staircase, the stair-builder can frame the carriage, confident that the finished staircase will have the correct rises.

Remember that before you actually start to build the stairs, it's a good idea to have the owner or designer's flooring choices settled in writing; any changes in materials should occur during the story-pole stage, when they can be easily accommodated. Once the stair carriage is framed, any change in the flooring thickness will mean a costly overhaul or a complete rebuild of the stairs.

Nowhere in the framing of a house is the possibility for accumulated error greater than in framing stairs.

Lon Schleining has built 500 staircases since 1978. He is the author of two books and numerous articles for Fine Homebuilding *and* Fine Woodworking *magazines.*

17

An Easy Way to Avoid Mistakes

Dotted blue line indicates height of ½-in.-thick prefinished floor. Double red line indicates height of plywood subfloor. Red line indicates height of framing.

Dotted blue line indicates height of 1-in.-thick tread. Red line indicates height of framing (stringer).

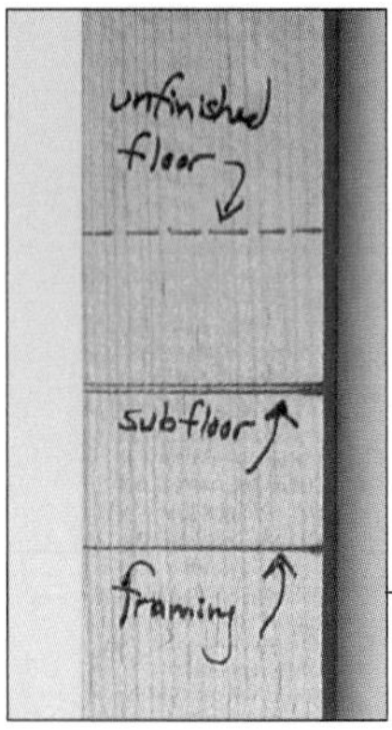

Dotted blue line indicates height of ¾-in.-thick unfinished hardwood. Double red line indicates height of plywood subfloor. Red line indicates height of landing framing.

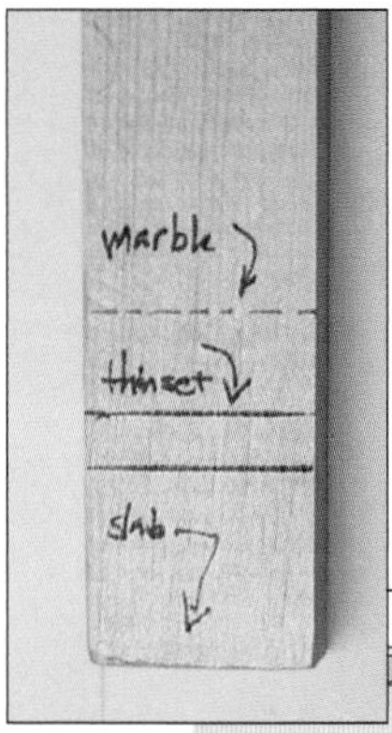

Dotted blue line indicates height of marble floor. Black line indicates mud base and thinset. The end of the board registers on the first subfloor or slab.

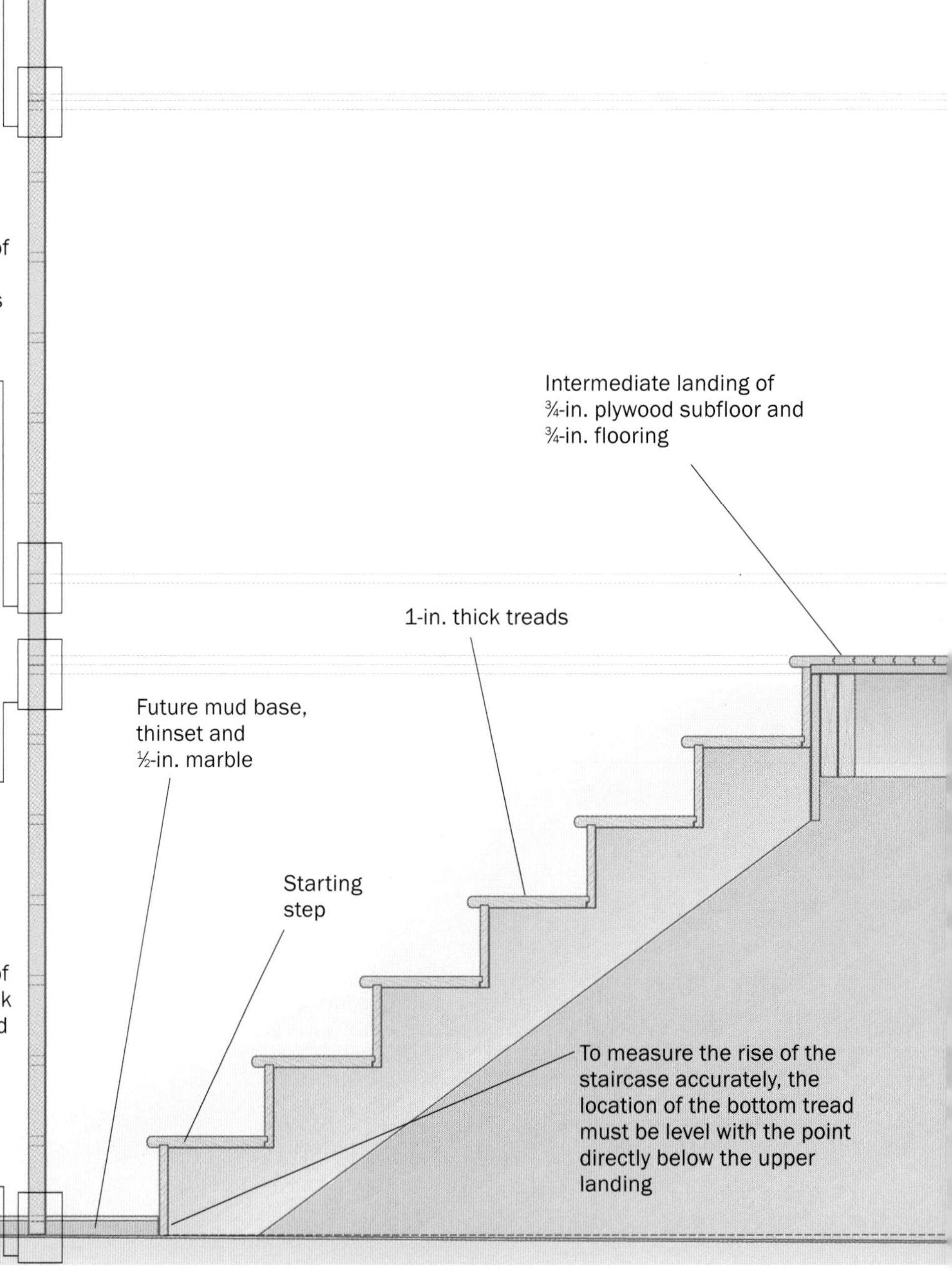

Finish-floor and tread materials of differing thicknesses often complicate stairbuilding. This story pole is a full-scale drawing compressed onto a thin piece of wood that allows a stairbuilder to calculate a staircase's rise and to take variables into account. The first line to be drawn on the story pole shows the second-floor subfloor elevation. Next, lines are drawn to show the finish-floor heights. The distance between these two marks is the total rise of the stairs. The total rise is divided by an estimated number of risers, and the intervals are fine-tuned with a set of dividers.

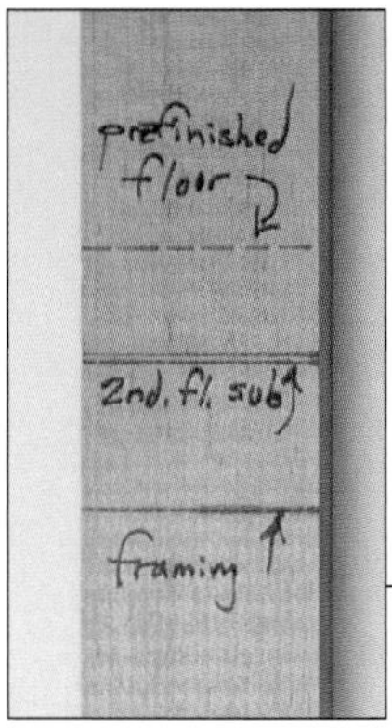

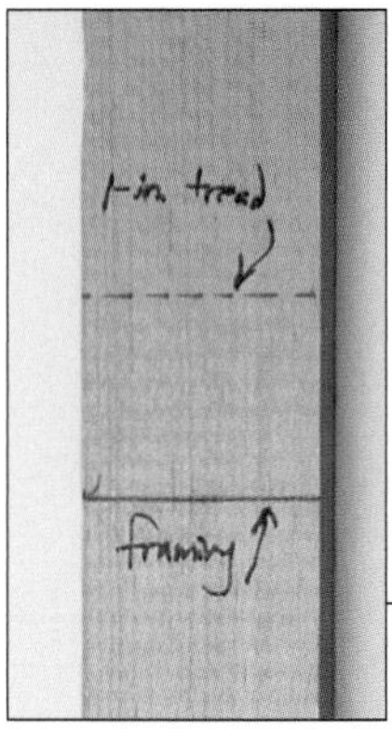

Intermediate landing of ¾-in. plywood subfloor and ¾-in. flooring

1-in. thick treads

Future mud base, thinset and ½-in. marble

Starting step

To measure the rise of the staircase accurately, the location of the bottom tread must be level with the point directly below the upper landing

(Story pole labels: prefinished floor, 2nd. fl. sub, framing, 1-in. tread, framing, unfinished floor, subfloor, framing, marble, thinset, slab)

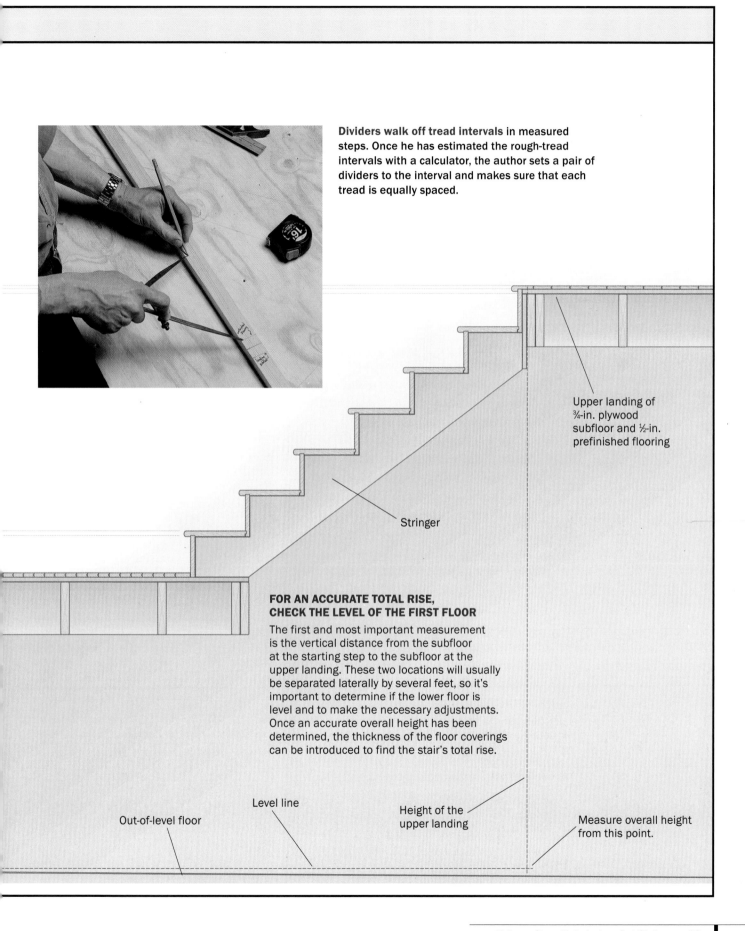

Dividers walk off tread intervals in measured steps. Once he has estimated the rough-tread intervals with a calculator, the author sets a pair of dividers to the interval and makes sure that each tread is equally spaced.

Upper landing of ¾-in. plywood subfloor and ½-in. prefinished flooring

Stringer

FOR AN ACCURATE TOTAL RISE, CHECK THE LEVEL OF THE FIRST FLOOR

The first and most important measurement is the vertical distance from the subfloor at the starting step to the subfloor at the upper landing. These two locations will usually be separated laterally by several feet, so it's important to determine if the lower floor is level and to make the necessary adjustments. Once an accurate overall height has been determined, the thickness of the floor coverings can be introduced to find the stair's total rise.

Out-of-level floor

Level line

Height of the upper landing

Measure overall height from this point.

Building an L-Shaped Stair

■ BY LARRY HAUN

Thirty-five years ago, orange blossoms scented the clear southern California air, streetcars hadn't yet surrendered to freeways, and the once-arid San Fernando Valley just north of Los Angeles was about to be transformed into suburbia by armies of construction workers. As the demand for housing increased almost daily, carpenters developed new techniques to keep up with demand.

A project I worked on back then was a 60-unit apartment house. Each unit had its own L-shaped stairway to the second floor, and each stairway had a three-step winder in it (a winder uses a series of wedge-shaped steps to make a stairway turn 90°. Not knowing how to construct a winder, I relied on my carpentry book for information. Using that information on the job the next day, my partner and I cut and built one set of stairs, but the winders alone took us more than five hours. Now, faster certainly does not always mean better, but that was simply too long. So we set out to find a winder technique that would combine speed with the quality of traditional carpentry techniques. The method we now use is quite simple and results in a stair strong enough to withstand the rigors of long service.

Merit and Demerit

An advantage of winders in a stair is that they shorten the total run, thereby leaving more space at the top or bottom of the stairs (see the drawing on p. 22). This is particularly helpful in small homes with limited floor space. Most of the winders I've seen are later carpeted, but I have also seen winders covered with hardwoods, even tiles, that look quite beautiful.

Whatever the surface, however, a stair with winders is not without danger. The fact that the width of each tread in a winder varies can present a hazard, unless you take care to step where there's enough tread width to support you. Building codes regulate the shape of treads in winders, though the codes vary from state to state. Some allow a winder to come to a point on one end of the tread. More often, however, codes require the tread to be 6 in. wide at the narrow end, or have a 9-in-to 10-in.-wide tread at the "line of travel," which is the path a person would likely follow when ascending or descending the stairs (see the drawing on p. 23). The line of travel is generally 12 in. to 16 in. away from the narrowest portion of the stairs.

Any stair should feature properly sized and secured handrails, but good handrails are particularly important on stairs with winders.

Traditional winder construction methods apply treads and risers to short stringers. Production methods offer a quicker approach.

First Things First

When building a set of stairs with a three-step winder, begin construction as you would with most any set of stairs. First, determine the total rise (the vertical distance from the first floor to the second floor). Divide the total rise by 7 in., a comfortable and safe riser height for most people. Round this number off to get the number of risers needed in a flight of stairs. Once you know the number of risers, divide that number in-

to the total rise. This will give you the exact rise of each step.

Here's an example. Say the total rise from first to second floor is 108 inches. Divide 108 by 7 and you'll get 15.4. Drop the fraction (.4) because it isn't safe to have a part of a step in a flight of stairs. Next, divide 15 risers into the total rise (108 divided by 15 equals 7.2). So in this particular flight of stairs, there will be 15 risers, and each riser will be 7.2 in. high (7⁵⁄₁₆ in.).

We set out to find a winder technique that would combine speed with the quality of traditional carpentry techniques.

A Stairway with Winders

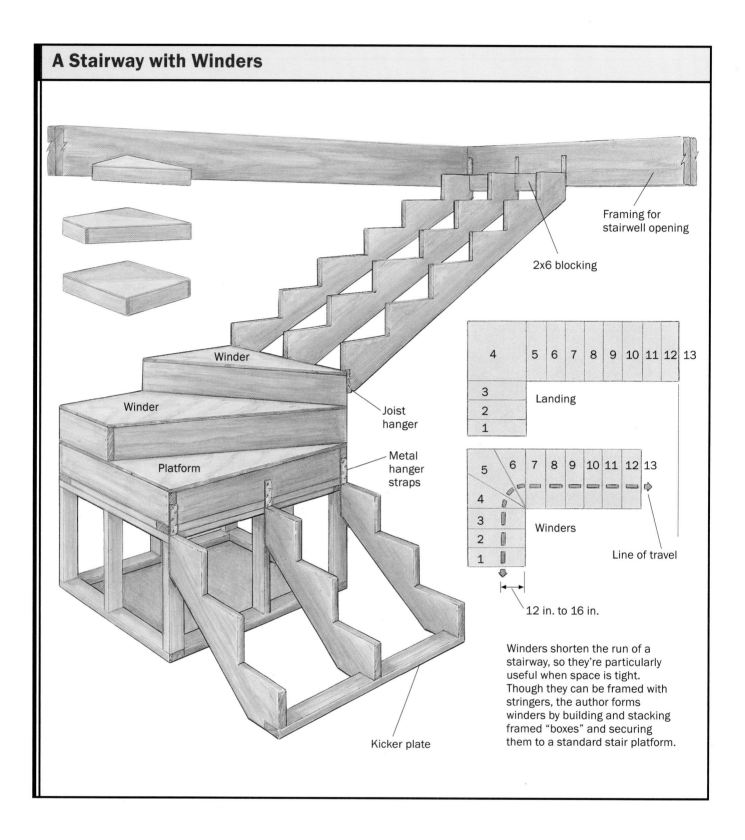

Framing for stairwell opening

2x6 blocking

Winder

Winder

Platform

Joist hanger

Metal hanger straps

4		5	6	7	8	9	10	11	12	13
3		Landing								
2										
1										

5	6	7	8	9	10	11	12	13
4								
3		Winders						
2								
1								

Line of travel

12 in. to 16 in.

Kicker plate

Winders shorten the run of a stairway, so they're particularly useful when space is tight. Though they can be framed with stringers, the author forms winders by building and stacking framed "boxes" and securing them to a standard stair platform.

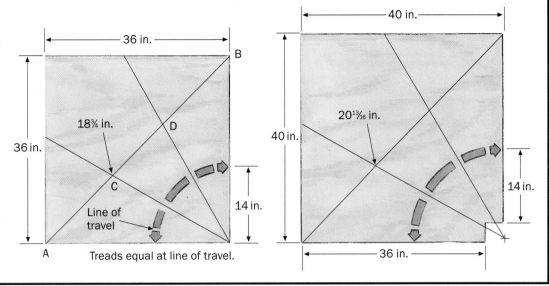

When laying out the treads, the key design consideration is to ensure that the treads are of proper width at the line of travel, which is the path a person would most likely follow when using the stairs. Building codes generally call for a 9-in. to 10-in. tread width at the line of travel. The methods at right can be used to lay out winders of various dimensions.

Building a Platform

Construction of the winders is straightforward and as easy as building boxes. The first step is to build the platform. Say that you are building a set of stairs in which the rise for each step is $7\frac{3}{16}$ in., the winder begins at the fourth step, and that the stairs are 36 in. wide. Frame a 36-in. square platform for the stairs and deck it off (before nailing down the plywood, I run a bead of construction adhesive along the top of the framing as a squeak stopper). The platform should be $28\frac{3}{4}$ in. high (four risers with a $7\frac{3}{16}$-in. rise equal $28\frac{3}{4}$ in.—simple enough).

Laying Out the Winders

Traditionally, carpenters have constructed winders by cutting out stringers, much like they do when building a regular set of stairs. This method is familiar across the country, and many of those staircases are works of skill and art. Production framers, on the other hand, eliminate winder stringers altogether; they simply build three boxes and stack them one on top of another. This is much easier than the traditional method and saves a considerable amount of time. The width of most main stairways is 36 in., so I'll assume that width in the examples to follow.

Start with a 36-in. square of $\frac{3}{4}$-in. plywood, and divide it into treads so the line of travel for each tread is the same. You can make the division using the "hit and miss" method, or you can use a more technical approach.

My hit and miss way begins with a line snapped across the plywood from corner to corner, from Point A to Point B (see the left drawing). Measure $18\frac{3}{4}$ in. on the diagonal from Point A to find Point C. Do the same from corner B to find Point D. Where did the $18\frac{3}{4}$ in. come from? After trying lots of dimensions, I've found that this one works to make a comfortable stair. Next, snap two lines: one through Point C and the other through Point D. These lines define the three treads of the winder.

The other method of laying out winders is more versatile and requires some arithmetic, but not much. Divide the 36-in. square piece of plywood diagonally as before. To find Points C1 and D1, multiply the length of the plywood by .52 (36 x .52 =18.7). In this

Production framers eliminate winder stringers altogether; they simply build three boxes and stack them one on top of another.

example, therefore, the distance in from each corner of a 36-in. square is 18.7 in., or about 18¾ in. Snap lines through the points you find to determine the winder layout. You can use this formula to figure out the winder layout of any size square or any width of stair. For example, if the stair width is 30 in., you would need to measure in 15.6 in. from each corner (30 x .52 = 15.6).

As I noted earlier, building codes frequently call for a winder tread with a width of at least 9 in. or 10 in. at the line of travel. If this is the case, you'll need a 40-in.-square piece of plywood to make the platform for a 36-in.-wide flight of stairs. You'll have to project the inside corner point far enough out diagonally so there is enough tread width at the line of travel.

Establish the 36-in. width of the stairs on the plywood as shown in the right drawing on p. 23. Then proceed to lay out the line-of-travel radius and divide it into three equal arcs. Connect points on the arcs with lines leading to the inner corner of the layout to complete the winder layout. This will provide a 10½-in. tread at a 14-in. line of travel.

Constructing the Risers

After laying out the risers on a sheet of plywood, cut them out with a circular saw. The rise of the step in our example is 7³⁄₁₆ in., so take some 2x8 stock and rip it down to 6⁷⁄₁₆ in. You might as well rip enough to do all of the risers—you'll need about 24 lineal feet in all. The ripped stock will form the actual riser of each step, as well as the "joists" that support successive steps. Once you nail the 2x stock together, sheet the frame with the plywood. Toenail this box to the landing.

Now take the smallest piece of plywood, the one shaped like a piece of pie, and build the last riser with the last of the ripped-down 2x8 stock. Toenail this box on top of the previous one. That's all there is to it— the landing is now a three-step winder.

Installing Stair Stringers

With the landing and winders complete, you can cut and attach the stringers for the rest of the stair. These stringers, both upper and lower, are laid out and cut as usual. A stringer from the first floor to the landing requires three risers: the fourth riser is created by the landing itself when the stringer is hung from it. Stairs that are 36 in. wide require three stringers—one on each side of the landing and one in the middle—and are usually cut from 2x12 stock.

One way to hang the stringers is to nail an 18-in. long perforated metal strap to the bottom edge of the stringers. This should be a heavy-gauge strap, not plumber's tape or the like. Nail the last 6 in. of the strap to the bottom of the stringer with four 16d nails. Then bend the strap around the backside of the top riser either by hand or with a hammer. The strap should extend above the top tread by about 6 in.

To locate the stringers on the landing, measure down 7³⁄₁₆ in. from the top of the joist and strike a line parallel to the edge. Hold each stringer to the mark, and secure it by nailing the end of the metal strap into the face of the platform with four 16d nails. The straps carry the actual weight of the stairs.

Next, nail a pair of 2x6 blocks (in this part of the country, we call them pressure blocks) to the platform and between the stringers. This block helps keep all three stringers stable until the stairs get their treads and risers. Secure the bottom of the lower stringers with a 2x4 kicker plate. This plate should be as long as the finished stairs are wide. Slip it into a notch at the bottom of the stringer and nail it to the floor.

Stacking steps. The winders are simply triangular or trapezoidal boxes made of 2x framing; plywood forms the steps. After the stair platform has been framed, the first box is toenailed to it, after which the second box is toenailed to the first.

Another way to secure the lower set of stringers is to use joist hangers. Using a circular saw, kerf the back side of the last riser. Slip the joist hanger into the saw cut and nail it to the joist and then to the landing.

After installing the lower stringers, you can install the stringers that run from the landing to the second floor. The top of each stringer is attached to the second-floor framing with metal straps, just as the lower stringers were secured to the landing. The bottom of each stringer is secured to the landing with a joist hanger. I cut 1½ in. off the bottom tip of each stringer, which allows it to bear nicely on a joist hanger. If the inside stringers are against a wall, we nail a Simpson® A35 framing anchor at the juncture of the stringer and the platform.

Securing stringers in this fashion is a tried-and-true procedure; we have been doing it for more than 30 years. The stairs will not come loose no matter how much the wood shrinks and no matter how heavy the load they're asked to support.

Larry Haun is the author of Habitat for Humanity How to Build a House, Homebuilding Basics: Carpentry, *and* The Very Efficient Carpenter, *all published by The Taunton Press. He lives in Coos Bay, OR.*

A Veteran Stairbuilder's Tools and Tips

■ BY MICHAEL VON DECKBAR-FRABBIELE

Judicious grinding of spade bits makes them bore holes in diameters between stock sizes. Beveled corners prevent tearout.

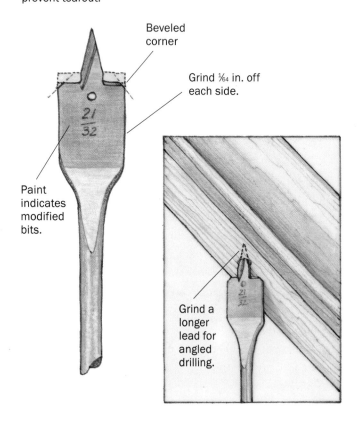

Beveled corner

Grind ¹⁄₆₄ in. off each side.

Paint indicates modified bits.

Grind a longer lead for angled drilling.

If you've ever poked around in an old toolbox, you're likely to have pulled out some strange-looking gizmo that, even after careful scrutiny, confounded all by its presence. Such tools typically elicit the comment "I wonder what they used that for?" As a woodworker who specialized in stairbuilding, I made plenty of special tools and jigs that'll probably end up as curiosity-provoking what's-its. These tools and jigs made my job easier, and, as someone once told me, it's not doing hard work that makes one a master, it's making hard work easier. So let's take a look at a stairbuilder's gizmos and at some techniques that should help you do a few things in your work: reduce effort, increase productivity, elevate your degree of accuracy and, ultimately, increase your profit.

Reground Spade Bits Work Better

The worst thing in the entire world that can befall a stair man is to hear his just-installed treads squeak. The second-worst thing is to have the spindles rattle. Children love it;

they never seem to tire of running up and down the balustrade with an arm extended, slapping the spindles to produce a staccato to which their youthful nervous systems seem immune.

For spindles not to rattle, they have to fit perfectly in their holes. To make a perfect fit, I modify common spade bits. It's easy to grind down the bits by $\frac{1}{32}$ in. (or $\frac{1}{64}$ in. on each side). So, for example, instead of jumping from $\frac{5}{8}$ in. to $\frac{11}{16}$ in., you'll have a bit that's $\frac{21}{32}$ in. (see the drawing on the facing page).

Another hint: Because the newly modified bits will have their former sizes stamped on them, it's important to paint new numbers on the sides of each bit. Once, a carpenter who was setting a balustrade went into my toolbox without my knowledge and bored 35 holes with what he thought was a $\frac{3}{4}$-in. bit.

Another thing about spade bits: When boring at an angle, say, into an oak handrail, a spade bit's 90° corners tend to tear out chunks of wood as they start a hole. Grinding off the bit's corners makes a clean cut by producing a scraping action as the bit spins into wood. I grind a long lead on some bits to make them useful for grinding holes in steep handrails. The long lead establishes the bit in its hole before the shoulder engages wood.

Shortened Level Fits on Tread

When leveling treads from front to back, it's handy to have a small level. You could buy a small bullet level, but I've never found one that didn't seem like a toy. I cut down a larger wood level to 10 in. and screwed small extension blocks of wood on the ends (see the drawing above). The blocks extend past the bottom of the level because sometimes a tread isn't exactly flat, so the extension blocks allow the body of the level to clear the belly of a chubby tread and give an accurate read. For years I used a longer 2-ft. level when I was setting treads, but I was

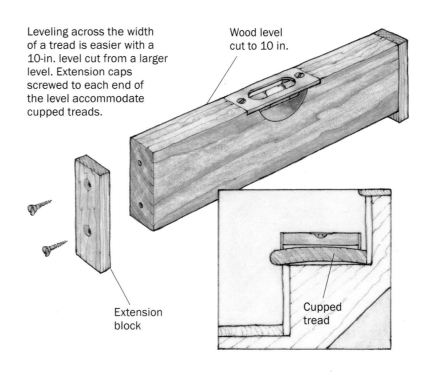

Leveling across the width of a tread is easier with a 10-in. level cut from a larger level. Extension caps screwed to each end of the level accommodate cupped treads.

Wood level cut to 10 in.

Extension block

Cupped tread

constantly bumping into the level where it was protruding past the tread and knocking it down the staircase. Aside from the fact that the tumbling level dented and dinged up the treads during its descent, I got pretty tired of buying new levels because the old ones got knocked out of whack.

Gauge Measures Shim Thickness

In many cases, the stair carriage (or horse, or rough stringer) is built by the framing carpenter, who is long gone by the time you come along to make a silk purse out of an old sow's ear. No offense to the framers; many do a great job. Nonetheless, it is in your best interest to build the rough stringers yourself, or at least check them with level and rule before you bid on finishing the stairs. It once took me three days with a reciprocating saw, a firmer chisel, and a mass of shim stock to straighten out a circular-stair string (pun intended) before I could trim it out.

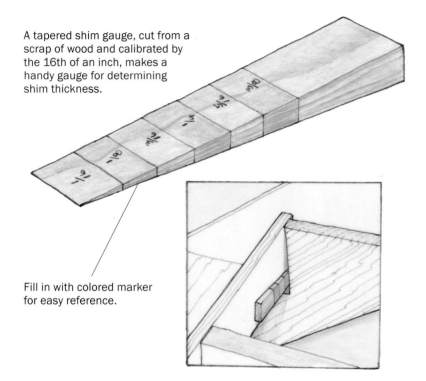

A tapered shim gauge, cut from a scrap of wood and calibrated by the 16th of an inch, makes a handy gauge for determining shim thickness.

Fill in with colored marker for easy reference.

I make a shim gauge out of a scrap of wood. I measure along both edges of the shim and make marks every $\frac{1}{16}$ in. in thickness (see the drawing above). I take a marker and color in everyother segment. After I've got the gauge made, I rip shims of different thicknesses and keep them on hand. Some people use shingles as shims, but their tapered profile gives them uneven bearing; the surface to be shimmed only hits the high point of the shingle.

To use the gauge, I simply slip it under the tread or behind the riser (see the inset drawing above) that needs shimming and tap it in until the tread is level or the riser is plumb. I note the mark on the gauge, remove the gauge, and replace it with one of my precut shims. Once you have the shim in place, the difficult work is done, and then it's just a matter of fastening the tread or riser to the carriage.

The whole process of shimming treads is slowed or voided if the center carriage is too high. When I cut my own carriages, I eliminate the possibility of the condition arising by overcutting both the treads and risers of the center carriage $\frac{1}{2}$ in. to $\frac{3}{8}$ in. By doing this I've eliminated the chance that the treads of the middle carriage will protrude past the line formed between the two outside carriages.

When it comes time to install the treads, I level and shim the two outside carriages. Then, it is simply a matter of gluing and screwing a 1½-in. cleat to the center carriage, which is brought into contact with the finish tread.

You can use the same process for the risers. By eliminating the center horse in the initial shimming process, leveling and shimming is transformed from a struggle into a dance.

Handrail Jacks Support Rails in Place

One day when I was scheduled to install a circular handrail, my helper didn't show up. To take his place, I made three rail jacks. The jacks are fairly complex, and they took a while to make. But they were well worth the effort: These rail-jack "helpers" are always on time in the morning, and they don't require a paycheck.

The jacks are made of a post and an elevator that ride along one another by means of a sliding dovetail (see the top drawing on the facing page). A piece of threaded rod, controlled by a T-handle at the top of the elevator, screws through a long nut (sold in hardware stores as a coupling for threaded rod) held captive in the stationary post. C-clamps at the base of the jack hold it to the finish tread. Short blocks of 2x brace the jack against the tread above. A diagonal brace, screwed to both the post and base of the jack, keeps the jack steady. Rail clamps are made of shortened pipe clamps.

When I installed the handrail, I used one jack at the top of the staircase, one at the middle of the staircase and one at the bottom of the staircase. When I am setting a circular rail, movement at any one of these three points is critical because any movement at one point has an effect on the other two points.

After using the jacks to ensure the rail is situated, marked, cut, and fit correctly to the newels, I use a jack or two to steady the rail while boring holes for the spindles. Because of their unwieldiness, circular rails must be bored in situ, unlike straight rails, which can be bored upside down on sawhorses by means of a pitch gauge.

I attach a level vial to my drill when I bore spindle holes; this ensures the plumbness of the spindles.

Reinforcing the First Step

Often, because the carriage at the first tread must be cut shorter than the unit rise to allow for tread thickness (usually 1 in.) and also notched for a 2x4 floor cleat, the bottom of the carriage is weakened. I always beef up the carriages by screwing and gluing a piece of plywood to the sides (see the bottom drawing at right).

Covering Newel-Mounting Bolts

Sometimes the only way to fasten the newel post is to anchor it to the rough horses. (For an alternative method of attaching newels, see "Making a Bullnose Starting Step" on p. 82) Often, the bolt holes you have to drill are at an angle other than square to the face of the newel. Off-angle holes can be hard to plug, and when you do plug them, they usually don't look right. Instead of plugging holes, I saw ¼ in. off the face of the newel with a bandsaw, drill and install the bolts,

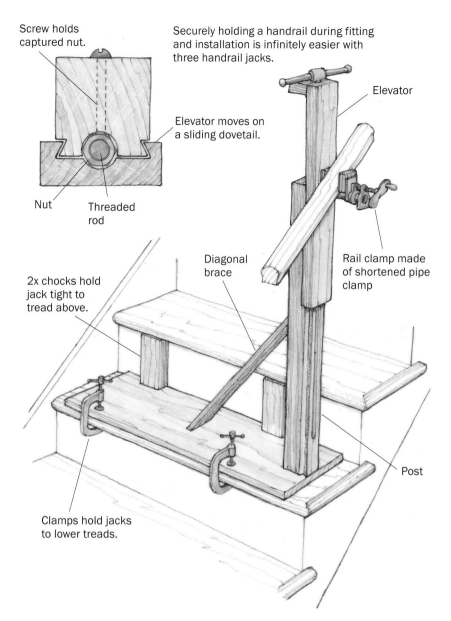

Screw holds captured nut.

Elevator moves on a sliding dovetail.

Nut

Threaded rod

Securely holding a handrail during fitting and installation is infinitely easier with three handrail jacks.

Elevator

Rail clamp made of shortened pipe clamp

2x chocks hold jack tight to tread above.

Diagonal brace

Post

Clamps hold jacks to lower treads.

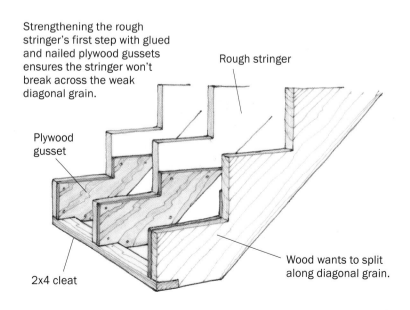

Strengthening the rough stringer's first step with glued and nailed plywood gussets ensures the stringer won't break across the weak diagonal grain.

Rough stringer

Plywood gusset

Wood wants to split along diagonal grain.

2x4 cleat

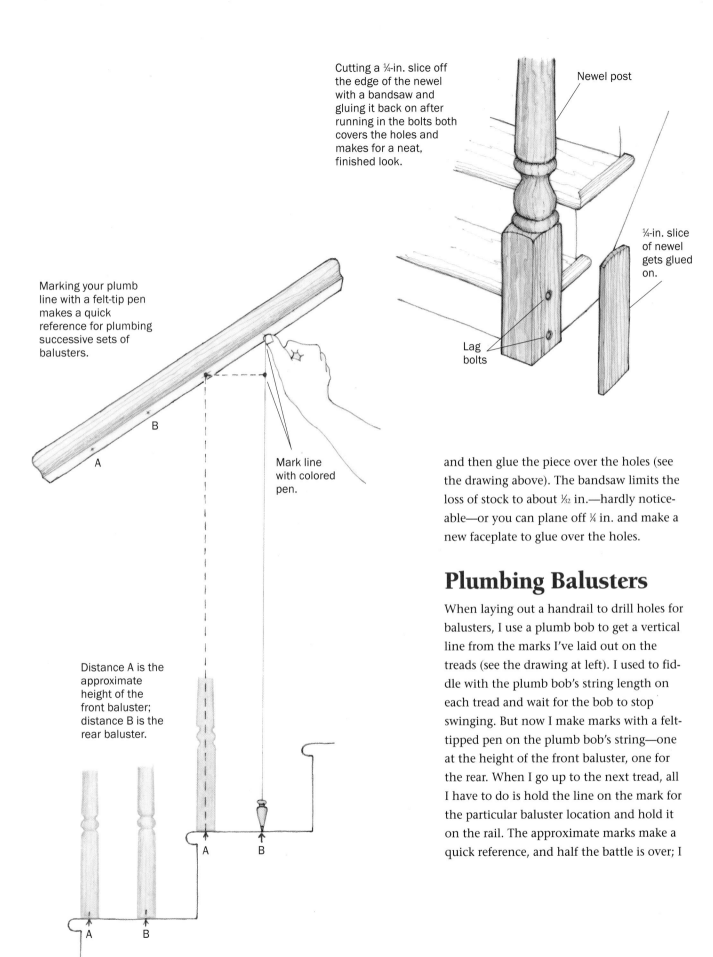

Cutting a ¼-in. slice off the edge of the newel with a bandsaw and gluing it back on after running in the bolts both covers the holes and makes for a neat, finished look.

Newel post

¼-in. slice of newel gets glued on.

Lag bolts

Marking your plumb line with a felt-tip pen makes a quick reference for plumbing successive sets of balusters.

B

A

Mark line with colored pen.

Distance A is the approximate height of the front baluster; distance B is the rear baluster.

A   B

A   B

and then glue the piece over the holes (see the drawing above). The bandsaw limits the loss of stock to about ½ in.—hardly noticeable—or you can plane off ¼ in. and make a new faceplate to glue over the holes.

Plumbing Balusters

When laying out a handrail to drill holes for balusters, I use a plumb bob to get a vertical line from the marks I've laid out on the treads (see the drawing at left). I used to fiddle with the plumb bob's string length on each tread and wait for the bob to stop swinging. But now I make marks with a felt-tipped pen on the plumb bob's string—one at the height of the front baluster, one for the rear. When I go up to the next tread, all I have to do is hold the line on the mark for the particular baluster location and hold it on the rail. The approximate marks make a quick reference, and half the battle is over; I don't have to fumble with string length. Here's another hint: I've found that using braided string, as opposed to the more common twisted-strand string, helps to keep my plumb bob from spinning and swinging around when the bob is hanging free.

Baluster Gauge

Some staircases call for square-ended balusters that fit into a groove plowed into the underside of the handrail. In an ideal world all the balusters for a given position on each tread would be the same, and you could just go along and cut sets of short and long balusters. For various reasons, though, baluster lengths can vary as much as $\frac{3}{16}$ in.

I made a baluster gauge that employs the sliding metal ruler taken from the end of a folding rule (see the drawing at right). The thin metal ruler is let into a piece of wood cut a couple of inches shorter than the shortest baluster. Small wood straps hold the ruler in place. A level vial let into the piece of wood makes plumbing easy. I secured the vial to the wood with Bondo®. The same measurements could be had by trying to juggle a level and a folding rule, but the time saved using this shop-made gauge more than makes up for the time spent making it.

Spindle-Hole Sizing Gauge

The diameter of the top, or thin end, of a tapered spindle can decrease as the spindle gets longer. Therefore, the hole drilled into the handrail for the back spindle on a tread can be smaller than the hole for the front baluster.

Baluster lengths can vary. On rails with a groove plowed on the underside, this gauge makes quick work of finding the proper length.

Gauge length is shorter than shortest baluster

Metal extension from folding ruler

Groove plowed in handrail

Level vial let in and secured with Bondo

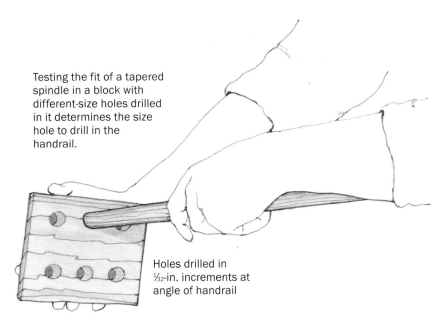

Testing the fit of a tapered spindle in a block with different-size holes drilled in it determines the size hole to drill in the handrail.

Holes drilled in ½₂-in. increments at angle of handrail

I take a block of wood and drill a series of different-diameter holes in it. The holes are drilled at the same angle that the spindles meet the handrail (see the top drawing at left). After I cut a tapered spindle to length, I plug it into the sizing gauge to determine which size hole fits best, then I bore the hole in the rail. To save time, it's best to have two or three drill motors chucked up with the bits you'll most likely need.

Circular-Rail Center Finder

For finding the center on oval or round handrails that have been fit and either permanently or temporarily fastened, I modified a marking gauge by letting a level vial into the gauge's beam and replacing the metal scribe with a pencil held in place by a wood wedge (see the bottom drawing at left). An auxiliary fence provides the additional height that is needed to compensate for the increased length of the pencil. By watching the level vial, I can keep the beam horizontal as I run the gauge down the length of the handrail, and I make a pencil line along its bottom center.

On a similar note, I've found that one of the most useful tools for both shop work and work in the field is a regular marking gauge with the metal scribe replaced with a mechanical pencil.

Michael von Deckbar-Frabbiele is a former stair-builder in New Orleans, LA.

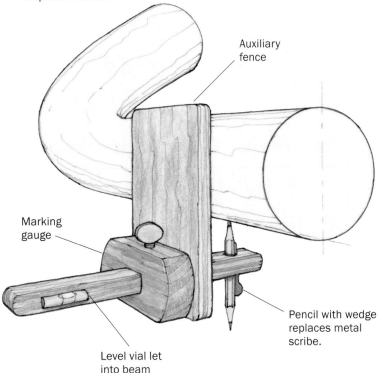

Modifying a marking gauge eases the process of finding the center of a circular or elliptical handrail.

Auxiliary fence

Marking gauge

Pencil with wedge replaces metal scribe.

Level vial let into beam

A Quick Way to Build a Squeak-Free Stair

■ BY ALAN FERGUSON

On a recent job, I overheard one of the young guys hanging cabinets in the kitchen say to his buddy, "Hey, who's the old geezer sitting on the stairs?" To my utter dismay, I quickly realized that there was only one set of stairs in the house, and the old geezer they were talking about was me. But thinking back on it, I have to admit that they were right. I've been building custom stairs for twenty-odd years, doing my own millwork and specialized handrails. As the years slipped by, I guess I have become that old man on the stairs.

But in the process of becoming this old stair geezer, I've learned a thing or two about building stairs, and I've reached a couple of conclusions. My first conclusion was that in order for a stairway to remain level, plumb, and squeak-free for a lifetime, it

An inexpensive stairway doesn't have to look cheap. Tread and riser end caps create a border for carpeting and a place of attachment for the newels and balusters. With shop techniques, even this economical stair can be built so that it stays level and squeak-free.

should be built under controlled conditions, such as in a shop.

With large stationary shop machinery, I can produce more accurate components that fit together to a T. Building the stair in a shop also means that I do all of my measurements and layouts in the friendly light and at the comfortable height of my workbench. Here, I can see my work properly to ensure accuracy. Too often on job sites, I end up working on my hands and knees on the floor. In the shop I always know there's an extra clamp nearby if needed, and there's no skimping or making do with less as I might be tempted to do on a job site.

On most sites, the handrail installer isn't part of the framing crew, so he's usually not around when the stairs are being built. But when I'm the guy who builds the stair and installs the handrail, I know where not to put fasteners and where to beef up the stair for extra strength, such as adding support for future newel posts. Another reason for not building a stair on site is that I always

feel I'm in the way of the other trades coming and going through the house, trying to get their work done.

One final plus to building a staircase in the shop is that I get to truck it to the site when it's finished. There's nothing more impressive than arriving at a site with a stair built as perfectly as a piano, carrying it into the house and nonchalantly slipping it into place. That's a sight that makes a hero out of any humble contractor in the eyes of a customer.

However, in spite of these advantages, most contractors in my neck of the woods like to build their own straight-run stairs on site. A guy like me could get mighty hungry waiting for a client or contractor to knock on the shop door to order a set of stairs. But I haven't been in this business all this time without learning to compromise.

So what about using shop techniques on site? That way, I have the advantage and convenience of building a plumb and level stair myself even if I can't have perfectly

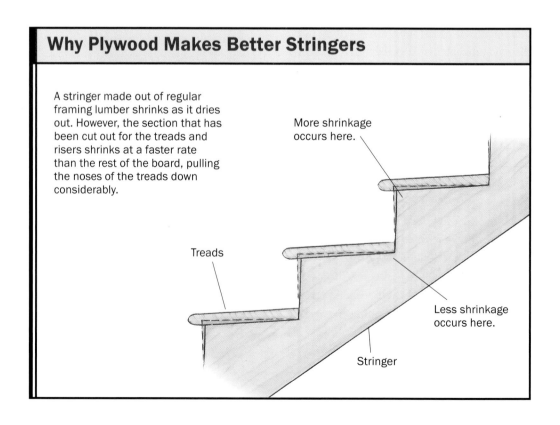

Why Plywood Makes Better Stringers

A stringer made out of regular framing lumber shrinks as it dries out. However, the section that has been cut out for the treads and risers shrinks at a faster rate than the rest of the board, pulling the noses of the treads down considerably.

More shrinkage occurs here.

Treads

Less shrinkage occurs here.

Stringer

controlled conditions. My straight stair design will give you an affordable stair that can be built either in the shop or on the job site for permanently level, squeak-free perfection just by following a few simple shop techniques.

Plywood Stringers Eliminate Sloping Treads

Something else I've realized from my years of building stairs is that stair stringers, or carriages, should be made of a dimensionally stable material, such as plywood, instead of 2x lumber or, heaven forbid, green framing lumber. Building stairs on a site where moisture levels change radically intensifies wood movement and shrinkage. Stairs made with plywood stringers are more likely to remain level and plumb as the house heats up and experiences drastic moisture swings from the curing of concrete and drywall compound.

Stringers cut from standard 2x stock will shrink unevenly as moisture levels in the interior of the house stabilize. These stringers shrink less at the inside corners of the treads and risers (the narrowest points of the stringer), and more at the outside corners where the stringer is the widest. This differential shrinking pulls the nose of the tread noticeably downward.

Stairs with sloping treads are dangerous, and as a handrail installer, I shudder at the thought of sloping treads. Making good baluster cuts to fit sloping treads is difficult enough, but cutting mitered returns for these treads and risers with any precision is practically impossible. Stringers cut from plywood don't suffer the same shrinkage problems, which eliminates sloping treads.

Materials Are Chosen to Fit the Budget

My stair design is versatile and can be adapted to almost any finishing style and budget simply by selecting different materials. The stair in this article was an economical solution for first-time homeowners struggling to stay within budget. Although they would have preferred hardwood treads, they opted for carpeted treads with exposed hardwood tread end caps (see the photo on p. 33). I cut the treads from off-the-shelf 16-ft. lengths of 1-in. OSB tread stock that come 11¾ in. wide with one bullnose edge.

Like the treads, the stringers can receive a variety of treatments, such as paint, veneer, or addition of a stylish trim. The stringers I used on this stair were to be covered with drywall, then painted, so I chose ¾-in. poplar exterior-grade plywood; however, any high-quality exterior plywood would have worked.

The risers were also to be carpeted, so I cut them out of ½-in. fir plywood. I always use kiln-dried 2x2 cleats for the riser-to-tread connections. I'm a stickler about using good-quality cleats to guarantee the best connections, so I buy baluster manufacturers' blanks that could not be used because of minor blemishes. Baluster companies are usually happy to sell me bundles of these seconds, called "sweet ones" in the industry, at a reduced price.

Two Layers of Plywood Form the Stringers

My first task was ripping the plywood for the stringers into 11½-in. widths. Using 8-ft. and 4-ft. lengths for each layer, I laminated two layers of plywood together to form stringer stock 1½ in. thick and 12 ft. long (see the photo at left), which I had estimated to be just long enough for this stair. Because the house was already weather-tight and because there was no danger of the staircase getting rained on, I was able to use one-part, shop-grade white glue with a 20-minute setup time. I staggered the butt joints of the short and long pieces between the layers and glued the butts with construction adhesive. If rain or moisture had been a consideration, I would have used an exterior waterproof glue.

I brought a big portable workbench to the site to give me a flat working surface for efficient clamping and gluing, but I could have easily set up a temporary workbench on site. Most guys would have skipped this step and done their glue up on the plywood deck, but the glue up is much easier to control on a good workbench.

For fast glue application, I use a fuzzy 3-in. paint roller with the glue in a pail. After spreading glue on both layers of plywood, I mated the top and bottom layers together and clamped them every 12 in. using C-clamps. I always double-check that my clamps are all tight, which means there will be no glue voids. While the glue was setting up on my stringer stock, I cut the tread and riser stock.

To determine the depth of my treads, I first had to calculate the width of the nosing. The end caps I chose for the treads came with 1¾-in. nosing, but the tread stock was to be covered with ½-in. thick carpet that my customer had selected. To make the overhang of the carpeted tread flush with the end cap, I added 1¼ in. (1¾ in. minus ½ in.) to my unit run and ripped the OSB tread stock to that width. Ripping the riser stock to my unit rise was straightforward.

Laminated stringers won't shrink or warp. Two layers of ¾-in. plywood are glued together for stringer stock that will remain stable and true for the life of the stair.

Leaving Out the Squeaks

When the glue had set, I unclamped the stringer stock and began my layout. Being careful to allow for pencil-lead thickness for each tread and riser, I laid out the stringer with my framing square and stair gauges (see the photo at right). Yes, I know it's a pain, but you'll thank yourself for making that extra trip out to your truck to get your stair gauges. Without them, it's impossible to duplicate the exact measurements from one tread/riser combination to the next. Just about or close enough at this point won't yield a precision stair.

For most stairs total run and width measurements come from the framed opening in the floor. Rise measurements are normally taken from finished floor to finished floor. However, these plans called for a landing with one step down at the start of the run. This detail meant that I needed to take my total-rise measurement from the top of the landing deck to the top of the second-floor deck. (For more on calculating rise and run for stairways, see "Cutting Out Basic Stairs" on p. 4).

The completed layout included the bottom foot cut where the stairs sit on the landing as well as the joist cut at the top of the stringer. The joist cut lets the stringer run up to the ceiling rather than end in an abrupt drop from the deck at the top of the stairs. I believe that attention to visual details such as this one is what distinguishes a craftsman's work.

Having determined the exact size of the bottom foot on the stringer, I gave the framer precise measurements for the height of the landing, which he began immediately so that it would be ready when I finished my stair. When the framer built the landing, I made sure that he glued and screwed every connection, which is the greatest factor in making squeak-free stairs.

Each tread/riser layout is duplicated exactly. Stair gauges clamped to the edge of a framing square allow the layout to be repeated precisely for each step.

I always add plywood backing to the top riser where the stairs attach to the upper deck. This extra layer of plywood helps to stiffen the stairway during installation and provides extra reinforcement under the nosing of the top landing. Because this small house was built with 8-in. rather than 10-in. or 12-in. floor joists, I cut a 2-in. deep mortise in the stringer at the inside corner of my joist cut that allowed me to use a full 10-in. width for my extra-plywood backing.

TIP

Add plywood backing to the top riser where the stairs attach to the upper deck. This extra layer of plywood helps to stiffen the stairway during installation and provides extra reinforcement under the nosing of the top landing.

Simple Jigs Speed Up Cutting and Assembly

Next I make a jig from MDF scraps to act as a fence for my circular saw to follow when I make riser and tread cuts in the stringer (see the photo on the left). The jig has a fence that registers against the bottom of the stringer, and I line up the jig with my lay-out, using a wooden block whose width is the same as the distance from the edge of the saw's foot to the sawblade.

Using a jig to make the tread and riser cuts is another shop technique most carpenters working on site would probably skip, thinking it too much trouble. But using this jig as a guide, I eliminate problems and imperfections that result from freehand cutting with a circular saw. My cuts with the jig are perfect, ensuring cabinet-quality joinery for the finished stair.

Because the circular saw doesn't reach all the way into each corner, I finish each cut with a jigsaw and then clean up the inside corner with a wide chisel. When the first stringer is finished, I clamp it securely to the second one and trace it to ensure an exact match. I cut the second stringer the same way as the first.

Now, with both stringers cut, I make a simple assembly jig that screws to two sawhorses (see the top photo on the facing page). This jig holds the stringers firmly and perfectly parallel at waist height. Here again, most of the guys I see on site either assemble the stairs on the floor, working on their hands and knees, or they assemble the stairs in place, struggling to fasten the treads and risers while keeping the stringers aligned properly.

Next I square one stringer to the other in the assembly jig using witness marks and my framing square (see the bottom photo on the facing page). The witness marks are made by

MDF jig for perfect sawcuts. The table of the circular saw registers against the edge of a simple jig made from MDF to eliminate freehand sawing. The cuts are finished with a jigsaw and fine-tuned with a chisel.

Assembly Jig Serves as a Workstation

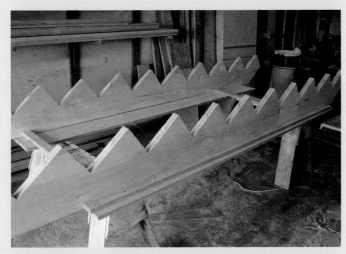

Assembly jig holds the stringers parallel and square. A simple jig made from strips of plywood holds the stringers at the proper width while the author is attaching treads and risers.

My assembly jig took a few minutes to set up, and it gave me a workstation at a comfortable height where I could keep things square and level. The assembly jig is made of two 8-ft.-long platforms mounted between two sawhorses. Each platform consists of a 3-in.-wide plywood cleat screwed to a 10-in.-wide base piece. These platforms are screwed to the sawhorses so that when the stringers are standing up against the cleats, they are at the desired stair width. Some simple spreaders between the stringers hold the stringers firmly in place against the cleats.

placing the stringers flat against each other and making a pencil mark across both of them at some point. Then, with the stringers in the jig, I line up both pencil marks using a framing square and an extended straightedge that leaves my stringers perfectly square to each other in the jig.

A note of caution here about stair width. When determining stair width, be aware of any compensations you might need to make for drywall or to make the stairs fit in the rough opening. This stair was being installed along a wall, so I allowed for a 1-in. space for drywall installation. I also had to ensure that the finished stair would fit the rough opening, so I subtracted an additional ¼ in. when figuring the correct distance between the stringers. This extra space gave me ample clearance to slip the stair easily into place in the rough opening of the second-floor deck.

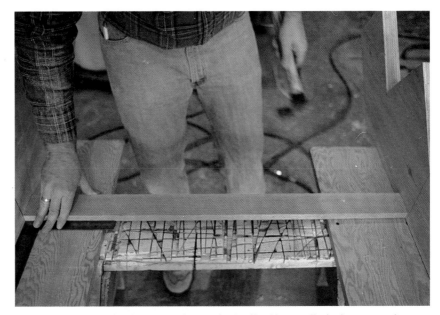

Witness marks help align the stringers in the jig. Lines called witness marks are made with the stringers laid side by side. Then a square and a straightedge align one stringer perfectly with the other.

Risers go on before the treads. For each step the riser is glued and stapled to the stringers ahead of the tread. Staples driven through the backs of the risers into the treads hold them together until the glue dries.

Staples Hold the Stair Together Initially

After the treads and risers were cut to length, the stair was ready for assembly. As I mentioned before, I always glue and screw all surfaces on all of my connections to ensure a squeak-free stair. Initially, however, I assemble the stair with a few staples, just enough to hold the elements together while the glue dries. At that point, I go back and add screws to every connection.

I start my assembly with the bottom riser. When it is glued and stapled in place, I set in one of my 2x2 "sweet" cleats behind the top edge to give me sufficient material to screw the tread into. Before putting in the first tread, I install the second riser and cleat (see the photo above). Then I glue the first tread in place and fasten it with one staple in each stringer and a couple of staples in the riser cleat. I also drive a couple of staples through the plywood riser into the tread, which has to be done from the backside of the riser. Following the same process, I staple and glue the rest of the risers and treads in place except the top tread and riser.

Top riser is reinforced for installing the stairs. The top riser is reinforced with a plywood backer that is screwed to the stringers from behind. A cleat will be added to the bottom of the backer board to support the top tread, and the nosing acts as a handle for guiding the stairs into position.

Screws keep out the squeaks. After the glue has set, screws are driven to fortify every joint and ensure a squeak-free stair.

At this point I preassemble the top riser and nosing together with the piece of backing plywood that fits into the stringer mortises I made earlier (see the left photo above). I hold this assembly in place while I lay in the last tread and staple it. This special beefed-up riser is one of the trademarks of my stairs. It not only stiffens the top riser for handling (and transporting), but it comes in handy when I'm setting the stairs in place.

Before removing the stair from the jig, I screw the treads to both the stringers and the riser cleats using 2-in. coarse-thread floor screws with square-drive heads (see the right photo above). I use these screws because they're beefier than drywall screws, so normally I don't have to predrill. In fact, the only predrilling I do is when I screw the top nosing to the top riser and backer. I finish the top assembly with a few screws through the backer into the stringer at the joist cut. I also glue and staple a 1-in. spacer strip (see the photo on p. 42) to the edge of the wall-side stringer.

Now I'm ready to flip the stair up on its side to screw through the back of each riser into each tread on approximately 6-in. cen-

A spacer strip allows room for drywall. A 1-in. strip stapled to the stringer will keep the stringer away from the wall studs so that drywall can be slipped in behind the stringer after the stairs are installed.

ters. As a final touch, I add a 2x2 cleat under the top tread against the ½-in. plywood backer where it extends down past the top riser. And the stair is ready for installation, barely six hours from when I started.

The Top Nosing Acts as a Handle

Ordinarily, a simple straight stair such as this one could be installed the same day. But those two young carpenters in the kitchen got so tuckered out just watching me whip up these stairs that I decided to postpone the installation until the next day when they were fresh.

The following day, I arrived to find my two young friends and the framer waiting to help with the installation. After double-checking the landing dimensions, we lifted the stair into place for a dry-fit. Now here's where that top-riser/nosing assembly comes in handy. I got on the top deck, and with three guys lifting the stair, I reached out, grabbed the top of the stair by the nosing and guided the whole thing into place.

The stair went in beautifully, so we took it back out to prepare for the final fit. I applied construction adhesive liberally to the joist header and under both stringer feet on the landing; then we installed the stair for good. My two crucial checkpoints were making sure that the 1-in. spacer strip was snug against the wall and that the top nosing was flush with the deck.

When everything was lined up properly, I quickly drove a nail through the top riser into the joist header to hold the stair in place temporarily. The guys down below could now let go and breathe easily while I took my time securing the stair through the

Ready for traffic. With the stair screwed in place and the step to the landing installed, the stair is ready for use by the construction crew. End caps and balusters will be added later during the trim stage. (Note: Insulation scraps made a great sound barrier for the wall behind the stairs.)

beefed-up riser with 2-in. screws. Then I moved to the bottom and angle-screwed through the stringer feet into the landing. Finally, I screwed the wall-side stringer to the studs with long screws.

In my spare time the day before, I built the single step leading up to the landing by gluing and screwing a box together using offcuts from the OSB treads, and I secured the step in place with screws and construction adhesive. The wooden end caps would be installed when I came back to install the handrail. And voilà, much to the relief of

the other subcontractors and to the joy of my customers, the stair was ready for use with a humble price tag but a picture of close-to-cabinet-quality precision and squeak-free perfection.

Alan Ferguson currently works as a kitchen and bath designer on Vancouver Island after a 27-year career as a designer and builder of custom furniture and architectural millwork. He resides in Qualicum Beach, British Columbia, Canada.

Hanging a Wall Railing

■ BY SEBASTIAN EGGERT

Building a staircase can be expensive and time-consuming. So when I tell my clients that they'll need a wall rail for the stairs to pass code, they often balk. Sometimes they ask me to install a cheap rail that they can remove after the building inspector has signed off. My response is that a permanent railing, built and installed properly, enhances the look of the staircase, and also that the railing might be all that stands between them and serious injury.

Longer Handrails Are Better

I begin the layout by setting a straightedge (a 4-ft. level works fine) on the tread nosings and lightly scribing the slope of the stair onto the skirtboard or onto the wall (see the photo on the facing page). Most folks like to be able to grab the railing before stepping onto the stairs. So at the bottom of the flight, I start the wall railing directly above the point where the slope of the stairs meets the floor. I find that point by extending the straightedge down the slope until it touches the landing. I then plumb up 36 in. from this point and make a mark on the wall.

I usually end the railing at least 3 in. beyond the nosing of the top tread at the top of the stairs. So I plumb up 36 in. from that point and make another mark on the wall. I then measure between these top and bottom points to get the rough length of the railing.

Locate brackets on studs.
A straightedge on the stair
treads determines the
slope of the railing.

Brackets Have to Be Screwed into Studs

A safe handrail is always screwed into the framing behind the plaster or drywall. In a perfect world, the crew that framed the stair chase would have installed 2x6 blocking on edge between the studs, parallel to the slope of the stairs and centered 32 in. above the slope. On rare occasions, I'm able to install the blocking myself. But in most cases, I have to hunt for the studs.

There are many framing-locator gadgets on the market, but I resort to one, only if I can't find any direct evidence of a stud. A nail hole in the skirtboard or a light joint-compound shadow where a drywall screw was covered are good places to start. Once I've located a stud, I transfer the stud layout up or down the stairs until I'm close to where I want to put the bracket.

I try to have the railing supported with a bracket as close to the ends as possible, so I hope to find a stud within 6 in. of the marks I made for the ends of the rail. If more than 6 in. of railing extends past the last bracket, I either lengthen the railing past the next stud or screw the end return to the framing. The UBC codebook specifies that the railing must be able to withstand 150 lb. of lateral force. So in addition to the end brackets, I try to put a bracket at least every 5 ft. along the rail for stiffness and support.

The railing I install most often is 1¾-in. dia. round stock that I make in my shop,

although the same procedure should be followed for hanging stock handrail and brackets. I mount the railing on brass rail brackets with round wall-mounting flanges and concave top saddles that fit the round handrail from Lavi Industries. If I put the center of the flange 32 in. from the slope of the stairs, the top of the railing falls at 36 in.

Let the Railing Align the Brackets

Next I measure up 32 in. from the slope of the stairs, and I mark that height on the centerline of the stud where each of the brackets will be attached (see the top photo at left). I start at the bottom bracket location by striking a circle slightly smaller than the diameter of the bracket flange using the mark as the centerpoint (see the bottom photo at left). I then center the bracket in place by viewing the circle through the screw holes that are in the mounting flange.

The bracket is rotated until the saddle is roughly at the slope of the stair, and one screw is driven to hold the bracket in place (see the photo below). I then repeat the pro-

Brackets are screwed to the wall. As the author views the circle scribed on the wall through the screw holes, the bracket is roughly aligned with the slope of the stair, and one screw is driven.

Plumb up the height of the railing at the stud location (above), and then scribe a circle for the mounting flange on the brackets (below).

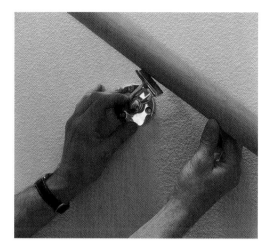

The bracket is then rotated into alignment with the rail (far left), and the remaining screws are driven into the wall framing (near left).

cedure with the bracket at the top of the stairs. Next, I lay a long uncut rail section on top of the saddles and spring-clamp it to the top bracket. The brackets can now be rotated slightly until the saddles are in line with the railing (see the top left photo above). Once the brackets have been aligned, I drill holes and drive the rest of the mounting-flange screws (see the top right photo above), making sure every screw hits a stud. While the railing is clamped to the brackets, I locate and secure intermediate brackets to studs, making sure the railing stays straight.

Don't Forget the End Returns

Now I can mark the exact length I want the rail to be, remembering to include the end returns when figuring the total length. Besides being required by code, returning the rail to the wall helps to prevent loose clothing and pocket-book straps from catching on the ends of the railing. With my railing system, each end return adds about 3½ in. in length and must be fastened to the rail beyond the end brackets.

After unclamping the railing from the brackets, I cut it to length with a chopsaw. I mark the center of the railing ends with a center-finding jig and a utility knife (see the middle photo at right). The end returns are joined to the railing with ½-in. dowels, and I use the chopsaw fence to align the drill bit

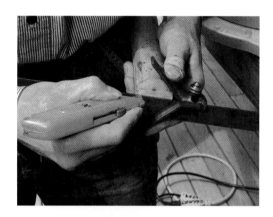

Drilling for the dowels. After squaring the ends of the railing, holes are drilled for dowels that attach the end returns. Holes are located with a center-finding jig (left) and drilled using the chopsaw as a guide (below).

End returns cut from a wooden doughnut. A semi-circular jig mounts on a chopsaw for cutting the 90° end returns. Lines on the jig keep the cuts at right angles.

Besides being required by code, returning the rail to the wall helps to prevent loose clothing and pocket-book straps from catching on the ends of the railing.

for the dowel hole (see the bottom photo on p. 47). I drill holes 1 in. deep using a masking-tape flag on the bit as a depth gauge.

The next step is cutting the end returns. The railing could be returned to the wall with a simple 90° mitered return, but I prefer the smooth transition of the quarter-circle. A semicircular cutting jig holds the shop-made

doughnut safely and lets me make accurate 90° pieces. I secure the jig to the chopsaw with the centerline of the jig aligned with the sawblade. Next, I make the first cut with the doughnut grain perpendicular to the sawblade. Then I rotate the doughnut 90°, lining up the first cut with the front of the jig and make the second cut (see the photo above).

Handrails and Code*

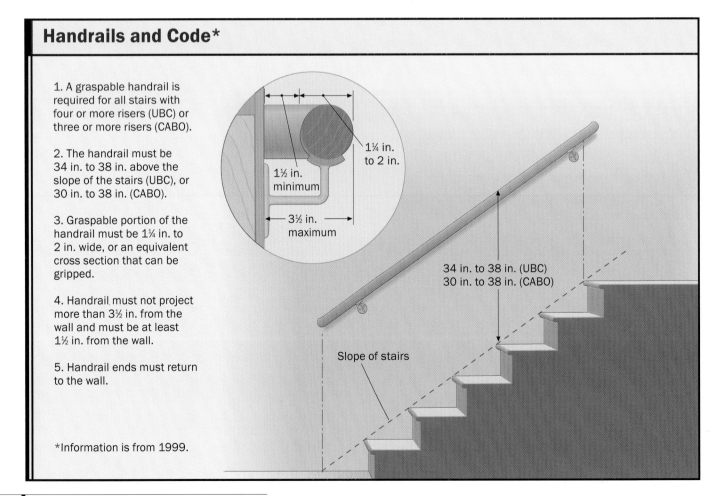

1. A graspable handrail is required for all stairs with four or more risers (UBC) or three or more risers (CABO).

2. The handrail must be 34 in. to 38 in. above the slope of the stairs (UBC), or 30 in. to 38 in. (CABO).

3. Graspable portion of the handrail must be 1¼ in. to 2 in. wide, or an equivalent cross section that can be gripped.

4. Handrail must not project more than 3½ in. from the wall and must be at least 1½ in. from the wall.

5. Handrail ends must return to the wall.

*Information is from 1999.

1¼ in. to 2 in.

1½ in. minimum

3½ in. maximum

34 in. to 38 in. (UBC)
30 in. to 38 in. (CABO)

Slope of stairs

I check the cuts with a combination square to make sure the ends are perpendicular. If need be, I fine-tune the cuts by clamping the quarter-turn back to the jig. By the way, I use this same jig for more sophisticated installations to plot and cut arc sections from the doughnut for changes in slope or direction.

Scribe the End Returns to the Wall

Next I spring-clamp the rail back to the brackets. Holding the end return with the grain lined up parallel with the handrail, I note the amount, if any, that the return sticks out beyond the line of the rail (see the top left photo at right). That amount is then removed from the end of the return that touches the wall.

Again using the chopsaw fence as a guide, I drill the end return for the connecting dowel. I insert a short section of dowel and dry-fit the return to the railing. Light pencil marks index the position of the returns to the rail (see the top right photo at right); then the rail is removed from the brackets for assembly and sanding.

I like to join the parts of the railing with a thick-consistency, industrial-strength cyanoacrylate glue, Hot Stuff Super T®. It is strong and dries quickly, especially when accelerator is sprayed onto the wet glue. I apply glue to all the mating surfaces, insert the dowel (see the bottom photo at right), and join the parts, keeping the index marks aligned. I then spray the glue joint lightly with accelerator.

I hold the fittings tightly together for a few moments until the glue begins to set up. The glue takes about 10 to 15 to cure fully inside the joint, so I handle the work gingerly during that time. After the glue has cured thoroughly, I sand the joints to remove

excess glue and to fair slight imperfections. In many cases, I also apply the finish on the railing before final installation.

Finally, I bring the finished railing to the stairs and hold it in place on the brackets, taking care to keep the end returns tight to the wall. The rail is then drilled and screwed to the bracket saddles. If I need to attach the return to a stud, I predrill and drive a 3-in. screw through the bottom of the return and into the framing. The hole can then be plugged and sanded. Before I leave, I always give the stairs and railing a test for comfort and for assurance that nothing has loosened during installation.

Sebastian Eggert is the owner of The Maizefield Company (www.maizefield.com), an architectural millwork shop in Port Townsend, WA.

Sources

Lavi Industries
27810 Avenue Hopkins
Valencia, CA 91355
(800) 624-6225
www.lavi.com

Williams & Hussey
Riverview Mill
27 Souhegan St.
Wilton, NH 03086
(800) 258-1380
www.williamsnhussey.com

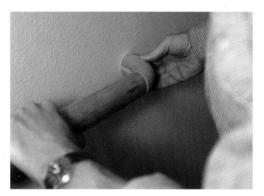

Fitting the end returns. If wall variations make the return stick past the rail (left), that amount is removed. The return is then set in place and indexed to the railing with pencil marks (right) for alignment during assembly.

All surfaces including the dowel are coated with glue (right), and the parts are joined together.

A Shop-Built Handrail and Fittings

There are a number of companies (including my own) that make and sell handrails in just about any shape and size you can get your hand around. But I get a certain satisfaction installing a railing that I've made myself.

Shaping the Railing

The stock I cut my railings from is 1¹³⁄₁₆ in. thick by 2¼ in. wide, and I make the lengths of railing as long as possible with a few extra 2-ft. pieces to test the setups.

Rounding over the edges of the railing can be done on a router, but I prefer to use a Williams & Hussey molding machine. With 1¾-in.-dia. half-round knives, the molding machine leaves a better surface. The stock slides through the machine on a guide-track jig that centers the 2¼-in. stock width on the knives, leaving a ¼-in. ledge on each side of the half-round shape (see the top photo at right).

I make several passes, cutting slightly deeper with each pass until the top surface is round. To complete the round shape, the stock rides through the machine on a second jig that supports the ledges created by the first step (see the bottom photo at right). The test pieces I made help to align the jig so that I'm left with a 1¾-in. dia. dowel when I am finished.

Time to Make the Doughnuts

I make end returns and other transitional railing parts from what your high-school geometry teacher would call a "torus." However, I use the same word that Homer Simpson uses, "doughnut." They are made in four steps (see the photos on the facing page).

The size of the doughnut is determined by how far the handrail bracket holds the railing from the wall. For brackets like the ones in this article, I make the outside diameter of the doughnut 7¼ in. The inside diameter is 3¾ in., and the cross-sectional diameter is 1¾ in., the same as the handrail. With the radius slightly larger than needed for the return, I can usually get four quarter-turns from each doughnut, allowing for saw kerfs and irregular wall surfaces during installation.

Railing takes shape. Square stock is fed through a molding machine that cuts a half-round profile.

The ledges left on the sides guide the stock while completing the round shape.

Step 1: I start with wood blocks 1¾ in. thick and 7½ in. square. At the center of each block, I draw a 3½-in.-dia. circle with a compass. On a drill press, I drill a series of 1-in. holes just inside the circle. The 1-in. holes reduce the resistance for the 3¾-in. drill bit that makes the finished hole, but the centerpoint is left for the center spur on the bit to follow.

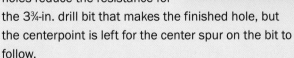

Step 2: I use a table saw to cut the outside of the blocks to a circle. The block is quick-clamped to a jig with a wooden disk on top and a guide strip for the saw table on the bottom. The edge of the disk is set exactly 1¾ in. from the table-saw blade.

1. Cut the inside hole. After a drill removes some meat in several small holes, a large spur bit in a drill press completes the inside hole.

2. Cut the outside circle. A special jig holds the block while the table saw cuts off the corners (left). The blade is then raised slowly while the block is rotated to round the outside edge (below).

I gradually slice the corners off the block with full passes past the blade, turning the block into a polygon that is close to being a circle. I then lower the sawblade and clamp the jig to the table beside the blade. With the saw running, I rotate the block on the jig, raising the blade about ⅛ in. for every rotation, leaving a smooth, circular outside edge.

Step 3: Next, I chuck a ⅞-in. roundover bit with a top guide bearing into my router table. I slip the round blank onto a jig with a tapered center plug that friction-fits into the doughnut's hole, and I round-over the outside of the stock top and bottom.

Step 4: To round-over the inside hole, I put the doughnut into another jig that holds the doughnut between four blocks using tapered wedges. The inside roundover completes the shape.

3. Rounding over the outside edges. A jig with a tapered center plug (left) holds the doughnut securely while a roundover bit in a router cuts the profile (right).

4. Round over the inside edges. Tapered wedges hold the doughnut in a jig that lets the author keep his hands above the work while rounding over the inside edges.

1. Cut the inside hole.

2. Cut the outside circle.

3. Round over the outside edges.

4. Round over the inside edges.

Building a Custom Box Newel

■ BY LON SCHLEINING

One basic shape provides a strong anchor for the balustrade and a variety of design options. The telescoping shape of this newel can be adapted to a range of styles that include flat recessed panels (inset photo) and more detailed raised panels, flutes, and moldings.

I n my work as a stairbuilder, I've always liked to build box newels: Their design is flexible enough to accommodate a range of styles, they're strong, and they are relatively simple to build. Unlike solid 4x4 posts that are clad with trim, these hollow boxes won't split their seams when humidity changes, and they're easier to install plumb. In the following pages, I'll demonstrate a straightforward way to cut, assemble and decorate these functional boxes. I'll concentrate on the starting newel because it embodies all the qualities of a box newel and none of the complications that arise as the balustrade ascends the stairs.

A Drawing Helps You and the Client

No matter what style you're after, you should put your thoughts on paper, or as I did in this case, a piece of scrap melamine. A full-scale drawing makes a great way to communicate the final look of a newel's flute sizes or molding details to the client, and more important, it allows you to organize your work.

In terms of a particular style, I like to start with a newel post that's built like a tree, larger at the base and more slender at the top. The post looks substantial. It's easy to attain this look by building a box within a box that telescopes upward.

The applied details depend on the situation. Plain flat-sided newels are handsome, but your client's house might need something a bit more ornate. Recessed flat panels, raised panels, carvings, flutes, applied moldings, and different caps all offer a way to express different styles.

Just about any solid wood works great for a box newel post; I use poplar for paintgrade stock and any number of other woods for stain grade. Construction is the same regardless of species, but when choosing materials for the newel, a chief consideration is wood movement. Keep all the grain running the same direction, lengthwise on the post.

Full-size drawing makes design an easier process. On a piece of scrap melamine, the author draws a detailed elevation and cross section of the newel, which allows him to plan carefully and to give the client a good indication of the newel's proportions.

Frame assembly is first. Prior to mitering, each side must be glued up. Splines of ¼-in. plywood secure the rails to the stiles. Flat or raised panels that fit into ¼-in. wide grooves must not be glued to the frame to allow the wood to react to climatic change.

I use medium-density fiberboard occasionally, but only for painted raised panels; it's harder to glue without resorting to biscuits. Plywood works well for paint-grade applications, but there are two things to consider. One, the lengthwise miter joints that I use to assemble the newels are not as strong as those with solid lumber. (This problem can be solved to some degree with splines.) Two, any exposed edges have to be covered, which always adds an extra step or two. For those reasons, I usually opt for solid wood.

Once I've chosen the wood, I plan the box. A newel of unadorned flat sides needs no further preparation now, but a frame of rails and stiles that captures a panel (flat or raised) needs to be assembled before you can cut the miters.

There Are Lots of Ways to Join Wood, but I Like Miters

You can use one of three basic methods of joinery to put these boxes together: miters, rabbets, or butt joints. Each method has advantages and drawbacks. Butt and rabbet joints offer a quick way to make boxes, but sometimes, the joint on the face of the

newel will eventually show through the paint. If the newels are clear-finished, there can be an obvious change in color and grain pattern at the joint. Butt joints can also be tricky to glue up without a jig of some kind, so I don't recommend them. Rabbet joints go together a little more easily than butt joints and are quite strong. Like butt joints, rabbets are usually glued and nailed, but their interlocking joints make assembly a bit easier.

Miters offer a quick way to build up a box without nails and to eliminate the unsightly difference in pattern and color between face and edge grain. If I use splines, I can also use plywood as a stain-grade option. With any material, the trick is to cut just beyond 45°, undercutting the inner portion of the miter so that when the box goes together, the outside corners are tight (see the photo below).

On a table saw, especially one that tilts left away from the fence, cutting miters such as this one is not much different from any other rip cut. If your saw tilts to the right, you can move the fence to the left of the blade. This position may feel awkward, but as with any new saw setup, I recommend a couple of dry runs with the saw turned off to get the feel for hand positions and stock movement. If a sequence doesn't feel right, find another way that feels safer. Having a tuned-up saw, a sharp blade that runs dead parallel to the rip fence, and an outfeed table will make any of these cuts infinitely safer. Cutting miters with a circular saw that's registered against a straightedge is a bit trickier, but the results can be nearly as good if you're careful.

To avoid grain or veneer tearout, I make sure that the sawblade cuts through the exposed miter edge first. Table-saw blades rotate down through the stock, so a left-tilting saw automatically cuts the outside edge of the miter on the top; if you have a right-tilt saw, moving the fence to the left of the blade does the same. A circular saw cuts up through the stock, so you need to keep the miters face down.

Undercut miters for a tight joint. Cut at 45½°, the assembled miters are open at the back but closed at the outside edge. The relieved miter takes less pressure to close, making it ideal to use with the tape method.

Aligning the rails. Before the author assembles the mitered sides, the panels for the box newel must be aligned. A framing square along the bottom rails does the trick.

Applying tape. With adjacent miters' outer edges touching, stranded packing tape is applied at regular intervals across the fronts of all four sides.

Gluing the miters. After the panels are flipped over as a single unit onto their faces, glue is applied evenly across the miters.

Assembling the Boxes with Tape and Glue

To glue up a two-tiered box, I first lay the longest set of mitered pieces face up along the bench (see the photos above and right). I stick stranded packing tape across the faces every few inches and leave enough excess to close the box. After flipping the assembly over, I spread glue onto the mitered surfaces and roll up the assembly. Ordinarily, the tape provides plenty of pressure for a good joint with no additional clamping; I'll check the box to make sure that it's square and set it aside to dry.

Sometimes, it takes more pressure than tape can supply to close the joints, especially if the pieces are not exactly straight, so I use a couple of bar clamps and mitered corner blocks that keep the sharp corners from becoming dented. As I check the box with my combination square, I can tighten the clamp to adjust one way or another.

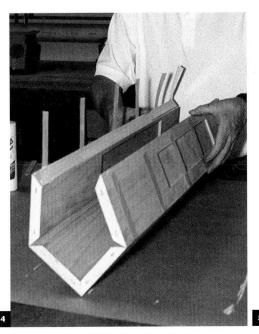

Creating a box. With the rails aligned and the glue spread, the sides are rolled up tightly. Long strips of tape wrap around the assembly and secure it.

Clamps and corner blocks square the box. While the glue is wet, the author makes sure the box is square. Squeezing the corners with a bar clamp allows fine adjustments.

A Router Jig for Cutting Flawless Flutes

Flutes on a newel post can add a nice detail to an otherwise flat panel. On this post, I wanted five flutes that were evenly spaced across the newel faces. I had to cut 20 flutes per post for three or four posts, so I needed a jig.

Made from a piece of ⅜-in. plywood, the jig is registered on the face of the newel by blocks (see the left photo below) nailed to the back of the plywood. Stop blocks contain the router's travel; spacer blocks, cut as wide as the distance between the flute centerlines, determine the location of the flutes. By moving the spacer blocks from one side of the jig to the other as I plunge-cut (see the middle and right photos below), I have equal spacing.

To design the jig, I first drew the width of the newel face on the plywood and then located the flutes equidistant across the face, drawing them to length as well. Next, I measured from the cutting edge of the router bit to the outside of the router's base plate and used that measurement to determine the perimeter of the stop blocks. Once the lines were drawn on the plywood, I glued and nailed the stop blocks in place. The glue ensured

that they wouldn't get knocked out of alignment when I was using the jig.

Before I get to work, I check the fit of the blocks and the router base. There should be about a ¹⁄₁₆-in. space between the router base and the jig so that there's no chance of the router binding. I always try out this kind of jig on a piece of scrap first, just to get warmed up and to make sure the result is what I want. I also try to buy a new fluting bit when I have a fairly large job; the bit is only $20 or so, a small price to pay for a nice cut. If you can avoid having to sand out burn marks left by a dull bit, the new one soon pays for itself.

I clamp the jig securely to the workpiece. A vacuum hooked up to the router's dust port will help to keep the jig's interior clean and to avoid chip buildup. With the spacer blocks all to one side, I plunge the router into the cut. (The first time you use the jig, you'll be cutting through the plywood jig and into the actual material below at the same time.) I move one of the spacer blocks over to the other side of the cut, one at a time, making sure to clean out any stray shavings that might move the block out of position.

Move a block, make another cut.
For each successive cut, one spacer block is moved to the other side of the jig. A vacuum keeps the jig clear of chips.

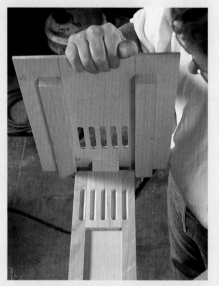

Stop blocks keep the jig in place. Glued and nailed to the back of the jig, these blocks register the jig in the same location for each newel face.

Spacers keep the router bit on track. The first plunge-router cut is made with the loose spacer blocks all to one side of the jig.

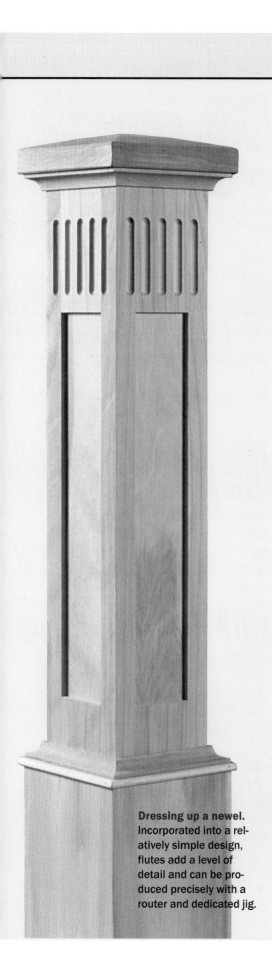

Dressing up a newel. Incorporated into a relatively simple design, flutes add a level of detail and can be produced precisely with a router and dedicated jig.

Assembling a box over a box to make the newel base. The second level of the box is built over the first; glue is applied to miters and to the interior faces of the sides. It's important to keep the grain direction running the length of the post to avoid split or cracked joints later.

I take off the clamps and tape after an hour or so. When the glue has set, I scrape the excess from the corners and sand any excess flat with a belt sander.

Using the narrower box as a guide, I then cut the pieces for the larger box and dry-fit them around the base, making sure that the miters are tight and that the grain orientation of the two boxes is similar. I apply liberal amounts of glue to the miters and inside surfaces of the pieces (see the photo above) and wrap them around the assembled box. I then tape the pieces together, using clamps if necessary.

Bolting the newel from the interior makes a clean installation. Hanger bolts driven into the landing come up through a platform that's glued into the bottom of the post. A universal-drive socket wrench attached to a 4-ft.-long pipe seats the nuts and washers.

Stock Moldings Provide the Details

I incorporate moldings of all kinds into my box newels, making different combinations to produce almost endless variations. For instance, narrow band or base-cap moldings nailed onto the inside perimeter of a flat recessed panel can mimic the look of a raised panel. I also like moldings along the transitions of the posts; one favorite is a combination of ¼-in. by ½-in. bullnose parting bead and a cove molding (see the photo above). These applied moldings also work to hide the exposed veneers of plywood, which must be covered even if the newel will be painted.

An Elegant Post Cap of Solid Wood

The cap style that I prefer is shaped like the hip roof on a house. I start with a square piece of 8/4 stock and cut the initial bevels on a table saw (see the top left photo on the facing page). I clamp a short piece of 4x4 upright against the fence of a crosscut sled and clamp the cap stock to the 4x4. A bevel of 15° seems to work well here. Then I finish it off with a belt sander (see the top right photo on the facing page), paying close attention to the contour as I sand.

To dress the cap and hide the junction of cap and post, I miter and glue together a square of molding, often ¾-in.-wide cove. After I make sure that this ring will slip over the top of the post, I center it on the underside of the cap and pin it in place (see the bottom photo on the facing page).

Hidden Bolts Secure the Newel

To attach the newel, I typically use four 6-in.-long hanger bolts that attach inside each post (a hanger bolt has wood-screw threads on one end and machine threads on the other); the hanger bolts offer a way to anchor a hollow post in just about any spot

A piece of masking tape around the end of the socket keeps the nut and washer from falling out.

MAKING A CAP FOR YOUR NEWEL

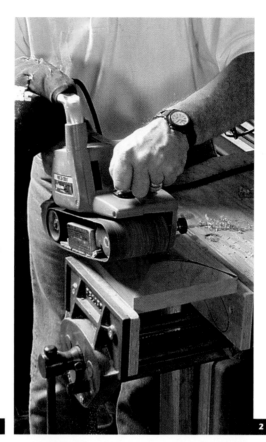

A belt sander makes the final shaping quick. After the cap's shape is cut, the contours are sanded. The cap gets a lot of hand traffic, so the surface must be smooth.

Beveling the cap safely. To make precise bevels, the author first clamped a 4x4 to the fence of the crosscut sled and then clamped the cap stock to the 4x4.

Pin the cap molding. The author preassembles the ring of cove molding and nails it without glue to the cap, which allows the cap to expand and contract.

you'll need. A bolt platform glued inside the base of the finished post (see the top photo on the facing page) gives me a bearing surface for the nuts and washers. After I've driven the bolts into the framing, I transfer their locations to the platform and drill holes slightly larger than the bolts to assist in adjustment. When the post is in place, I take my long custom wrench, tape the washer and nut into the socket and bolt down the post, plumbing it as I go. After I attach the cap, I'm ready to start on the next post.

Lon Schleining has built 500 staircases since 1978. He is the author of two books and numerous articles for Fine Homebuilding *and* Fine Woodworking.

Building Finish Stairs

■ BY ANDY ENGEL

■ had often marveled at the seamless construction of finish stairs. The rounded, tapering mortises in the housed stringer seemed to be made by sorcery, or at least by expensive, specialized machines. Then, 10 or 12 years ago, I read a review of a stair-routing jig. This simple $132 aluminum jig was an epiphany, and I bought one the next day. I built a few sets of stairs with it but found its rise-and-run range was too limited. Frustrated, I made a jig from ¾-in. plywood. The store-bought jig hasn't been out of its drawer since.

It's Easier to Build Stairs in the Shop

Most finish stairs that I've built have an open, mitered stringer on the outside and a housed stringer, where the risers and treads are glued and wedged into mortises, on the wall side. I usually built them in my shop because my tools were all at hand. Shop-built stairs call for careful measurements. If built to the wrong size, they can take up valuable shop space for a long time before you find a house they do fit. Measuring for stairs and ciphering rise and run are beyond the scope of this article. See "Cutting Out Basic Stairs" on p. 4 for a primer on stair layout.

I make the stringers from 5/4 stock because I can get clear, long lengths of dried and surfaced material. Nominal 10-in. stock is plenty strong for the housed stringer, but I use 5/4x12 for the mitered stringer. Even so, the notches will weaken it so that it must be supported by a wall. The inside of this wall is usually flush with the edge of the stairwell, and it's typically built after the stair is set. Plan the stair width so that the mitered stringer overhangs the wall enough for drywall to slide behind it.

The treads and stringers on this stair are 5/4x12 yellow pine. Where I worked in New Jersey, it's sold in lengths from 6 ft. to 16 ft., bullnosed for use as stair tread. It also makes good stringers; it's strong, and it's usually the least expensive clear pine available. When using it for stringers, I simply rip the stock to width on my table saw and save the rippings for tread returns.

Mitering the Treads and Risers

I usually make the risers from 1x10 or 1x8 stock, depending on which generates the least scrap. I first square-cut the risers about an inch oversize. This way, I can look at

Gang-cutting the treads for mitered returns. The author clamps all the treads together with their edges flush and square. He then screws a scrap-wood guide to their end. With the saw set at 45° and its cutting depth at the return width, he miters all the treads with one cut.

Trimming the tread to the miter. A framing square guides the circular saw, and the cut is finished with a handsaw.

Laying Out the Housed Stringer

After the mitered stringer is laid out, its top is held against the bottom of the housed stringer.

1. The housed stringer is marked as shown in the drawing. These notations are index marks to keep the tread-and-riser intersections consistent between the stringers and to avoid accumulated error.

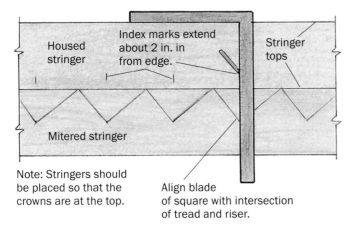

Housed stringer

Index marks extend about 2 in. in from edge.

Stringer tops

Mitered stringer

Note: Stringers should be placed so that the crowns are at the top.

Align blade of square with intersection of tread and riser.

2. To position the stair gauges on the square, the blade of the framing square is lined up on top of a tread layout on the mitered stringer. Its tongue is then slid 1½ in. past the riser line, and the stair gauges are affixed.

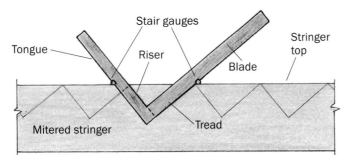

Stair gauges

Tongue

Riser

Blade

Stringer top

Mitered stringer

Tread

3. The author butts the stair gauges to the housed stringer, and he aligns the riser and tread dimensions with the first set of index marks. He then marks the outside of the square on the stringer with a pencil. The square is moved to the next set of index marks, and the process is repeated. Don't reverse the square—the layout would then be upside down.

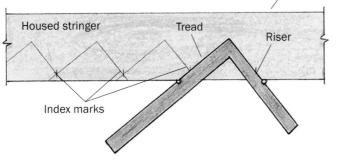

Stringer top

Housed stringer

Tread

Riser

Index marks

them individually and decide which edge to trim when I rip the risers to width. Then I set the table-saw fence to the riser dimension and rip all but two risers to width.

The bottom riser is one tread thickness narrower than the others so that the first step will be consistent with the rest. The top riser is generally ¼ in. wider than the others because the top landing tread is a transition between the stairs and the finish flooring. In my area, lumberyards commonly stock landing treads that are 3½ in. wide and have a 1-in.-thick nose that matches the treads. Their backs are rabbeted to ¾ in. to match hardwood flooring and extend over the top riser to rest on the subfloor.

The risers join to the outer stringer with a miter. I mark the actual length on the risers and miter them, making sure that the crown will be up and the best face out. I use a 12-in. miter saw, but a radial-arm saw, table saw, or even a portable circular saw will do the job.

I select the flattest stock for treads to minimize the sanding required to make the return and the tread flush on top. I rip and crosscut the treads to size and then, for a stain-grade stair, miter the outer edge of the treads to receive the return. The quickest, most accurate way I've found to do this is gang-cutting (see the right photo on p. 61).

I stack the treads, crowns up, and clamp them in a square, flush-edged pile that stands on the ends that will go in the housed stringer. I set the circular saw at 45° and its depth of cut to the nosing overhang, 1¼ in. I register the saw against a straight piece of scrap screwed to the treads' end grain. The outside of the blade should just kiss the front of the treads.

After cutting and unclamping the treads, I square-cut them to the miter with a circular saw guided by a clamped framing square (see the left photo on p. 61). I stop the square cut just as it intersects the 45° cut and finish with a handsaw. The stock for the tread returns comes from the bullnose edge of the wall stringer. The returns are 1¼ in. wide, leaving a piece of 5/4 stock 9⅞ in. wide, plenty for the wall stringer. For the outer mitered stringer, I rip only enough to square the edge. Because notching will weaken this stringer, it should remain as beefy as possible.

I cut the return stock to length, 45° on one end and square on the other, 1½ in. longer than the tread width. I bullnose the ends of the returns with a miter gauge and a rounding bit in a router table. I nail the returns to the treads with two 6d finish nails, one near the front and one near the back, being careful not to nail where I'll later drill for balusters. I glue the return to the tread at the miter and for maybe an inch behind it, but no more. This practice allows the tread to move a little without cracking. I sand the joint flush after the glue dries.

Using a Square to Lay Out the Stringers

I look the stringer stock over for crown, bow, and best side. Crowns go up, bows oppose each other, and best sides show. I lay out the mitered stringer using a framing square and stair gauges. It's a standard layout, so I won't go into detail about doing it. The only difference from an unmitered stringer is that the layout represents the fronts of the risers, not their backs. But this doesn't require any changes. Simply set the stair gauges on your framing square to the rise and run, and go.

The housed stringer is a little different (see the drawings on the facing page). It's laid out from the bottom of the stringer, not the top. The layout lines represent the front of the risers and the top of the treads—you don't subtract a tread thickness from the bottom-riser layout because of this. And the treads and risers don't intersect at either edge of the stringer. Because the layout represents the tops of the treads and the fronts of the risers, the intersection of the treads and risers at the back of the step has to be well within the stringer. Otherwise, the treads and risers would hang below the stringer. And if they intersected at the top, it would look like a notched stringer.

Cutting the mitered stringer. After making all the riser cuts with the circular saw set at 45°, the author cuts the stringer for the treads with the saw set at 90°. A handsaw finishes the cuts.

Thoughtful layout can hide cosmetic defects such as knots in the stringers. I try to make knots fall in the notches of the mitered stringer or behind the treads and risers of the housed stringer. Now is the time to think about how the base molding will integrate with the stringer, too. I like the plumb cut to match the height of the bottom of a two-part base so that the cap continues smoothly from the base to the stringer.

Mitering the Stringer with a Circular Saw

I notch the mitered stringer with a circular saw (see the left photo above). You can clamp a guide to the stringer if you aren't confident of cutting a straight line. I set the blade square to make the cut for the treads and at 45° to miter the stringer for the risers. I finish the cuts with a handsaw (see the right photo above). If the mitered stringer is on the right-hand side as you look at the stair from the bottom, a sidewinder circular saw will miter the risers just fine. If it's on the left, you'll need a worm-drive saw.

I select the flattest stock for treads to minimize the sanding required to make the return and the tread flush on top.

Fine results from basic techniques. Using a homemade jig and a router to mortise the housed stringer, a journeyman carpenter can build stairs with the tools found in most garage woodshops.

Or you could use a handsaw for either side. I've done that, and it's why I now own two circular saws. I save the triangular cutouts and use them for glue blocks later.

Making the Jig to Mortise the Housed Stringer

I mortise the housed stringer for the treads and risers with a homemade plywood jig and a plunge router (see the photo above). The jig is made from a piece of ¾-in. birch plywood. The type of plywood doesn't matter as long as it's smooth on both sides and is free of voids. It should measure about 18 in. by 24 in. With a framing square and a pencil, I lay out the jig as shown in the drawing on the facing page. The cutout in the jig has to be wider than the stringer so that the bit isn't in contact with the stringer when you start the router. This extra space also gives the chips an escape route.

The backs of the mortises have to taper to take a wedge. For a 9-in. run, the wedges measure 8½ in. long, proportionately longer for wider treads, ⅛ in. thick at the point and ⁹⁄₁₆ in. at the butt. I cut the scrap from the risers into 8½-in.-long pieces. Then I cut the wedges from these on a 12-in. miter saw by setting it to half of the wedge angle and flipping the stock after each cut (see the photo on the facing page). You can use the same

A Jig for Mortising Stringers

Made from ¾-in. birch plywood, this simple jig is used with a pattern-routing bit in a plunge router to mortise the housed stringer. This jig works for 1-in. thick treads and ¾-in.-thick risers.

Stringer

1 in.

1¼ in.

¾ in.

Location of tread

Location of riser

18 in.

Location of wedges

Layout line

Routed mortise

Cutout in jig extends beyond stringer for chip clearance when routing.

1½ in.

1¾ in.

24 in.

A chopsaw cuts the wedges. The angle of cut is set to one-half that of the wedge, and the stock is flipped front to back after each cut. The author judges the width of each wedge by eye. It's important to stop cutting before your fingers get dangerously close to the blade.

technique with a miter gauge on a table saw. Don't get greedy. I stop when I've cut about two-thirds of it into wedges. It feels dangerous to do more.

I hold a wedge along the underside of the tread marking and trace it onto the jig, repeating this at the back of the riser mark. I keep the wedges back about ½ in. from the intersection of the tread and riser. The wedges compress as they're driven in, and this ½-in. space keeps them from hitting the tread or riser before they're tight. Ideally, the driven wedges should just touch each other. Extend these angled lines, and you're ready to cut the jig.

I clamp the plywood to a piece of scrap so that it doesn't splinter when cut. I drill the front of the jig with a spade bit that matches the radius of the bullnose (see the photo at left). Then I plunge-cut the jig with

Drilling a hole the same radius as the tread's bullnose is the first step in cutting the jig. The rest of the jig is plunge-cut with a circular saw and finished with a jigsaw. A steady hand is required; any mistakes here will telegraph to the finished stringer.

a circular saw (see the bottom photo below) and finish the cuts with a jigsaw. These cuts have to be good—any mistakes here will show on the stairs.

Mortising the Housed Stringer

I clamp the stringer to my sawhorses and hold the jig on the layout lines with two C-clamps. I work from the top edge of the stringer and from right to left. After the first cut, I start all the cuts in previously routed mortises at the corner where the treads and risers will meet. By starting there, the corner doesn't chip as it would if I finished the cut there. And the inevitable blowouts from the router exiting the cut happen behind the treads and risers where they aren't noticeable. The mortises should be about ⅜ in. deep.

I use a heavy-duty plunge router with a ¾-in. pattern-cutting bit, one with the bearing mounted above the cutting edges. I take at least two passes. Raise and lower the bit beyond the stringer and away from the edges of the jig—it's easy to ruin the jig accidentally. If you aren't experienced using a router and a big bit, you should practice on some scrap and learn how the tool handles. If you use heavier stringer stock, the mortises can be deeper. I leave at least ¾ in. of wood behind the mortise.

Gathering Wedges and Glue Blocks

It's important to have enough wedges on hand. A typical 13-riser stair will take 25. If it had a housed stringer on both sides, it would need 50. I cut the rippings from the risers into glue blocks to reinforce the tread-to-riser joint. They should fit between the stringers with about 3 in. to spare. Next, I trim the cutouts from the mitered stringer for glue blocks between the mitered stringer and the treads and risers. Trim just enough to make them right triangles with good, square-edged gluing surfaces. The miter saw does this well. I drill three ⅛-in. pilot holes through each block and countersink the holes so that the screws won't split the blocks.

I fill my nail apron with 1⅝-in. drywall screws and 8d finish nails and load the nail gun with 1½-in. nails. I fill a big squeeze bottle with wood glue and have more on hand. Expect to use at least a pint.

Glue and Wedges Lock the Stairs Together

With the housed stringer on a flat floor, I put the bottom tread and riser tight together in their mortises (see the photo below). I squeeze enough glue behind the riser to cover both sides of the wedge. Glue holds the stairs together and keeps them from squeaking. I use lots and don't worry

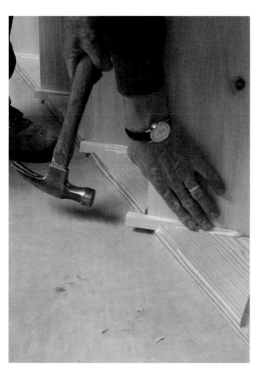

Wedges and glue hold treads and risers in the housed stringer. The glue should flow freely here. It holds the stairs together, and drips won't be visible from the face.

about squeeze-out here; it will be hidden. While keeping the riser seated in its mortise, I hammer in the wedge until its butt starts to splinter. Then I pull the tread out and install the rest of the risers the same way. The treads go in later. Keeping the risers and treads seated in their mortises is crucial. Their square cuts are what keep the stairs square.

The next step is easier with a helper, but not impossible alone with a nail gun. I nail the mitered stringer to the risers with 1½-in. finish nails through the miters (see the photo on p. 68). It isn't necessary to glue the miters. Glue blocks from behind will reinforce them with little chance of glue dripping on the finished surfaces. I keep the joints between the risers and stringer flush; otherwise, the returns on the treads may not fit tightly to the stringer. It's easiest to sand these miters before installing the treads.

Next, I run a bead of glue down the back of the first tread. I stay toward its bottom to minimize squeeze-out; it will show here. I put the nose of the tread in the mortise with its other end flat on the notch and rotate the tread into place (see the top left photo on p. 69). I check that the overhanging end on the return fits tightly to the mitered stringer. If it doesn't, I remove the tread and trim some from the housed end. Bracing the stringer with my body, I drive 8d finish nails through the tread into the mitered stringer, being mindful of where I'll later drill for balusters. Moving to the housed stringer, I spread glue in the mortise and then wedge the tread in place.

I make four dimples in the back of the riser using the tip of my screw gun as a countersink. The dimples reduce the splitting caused by the bugle-head drywall screws. I screw the riser to the tread with 1⅝-in. drywall screws through the dimples. I check the front to be sure the connection is tight, and if there are gaps, I add more screws. I wipe up any escaping glue and

Keeping the risers and treads seated in their mortises is crucial.

Putting the pieces together. Nailing the miters with a gun leaves one hand free to align the joint (facing page). A tread is rotated into place (below). Glue and screws from behind will secure it to the riser. Glue blocks (bottom) unite treads, risers and stringer.

proceed to the next tread. I leave the landing tread off for now. It's easier to install after the newel post has been set.

Before proceeding, I check that all the treads are flat on the mitered stringer. If any aren't, I screw an angled block to the stringer bottom for bearing, clamp the tread down, and add more nails. Then I wipe up any glue that's made a break for it since I last looked.

Gluing the Treads from Below

The treads aren't glued directly to the mitered stringer or to the top of the risers because I find this impossible to do without dripping glue on visible parts of the stair. Instead, I reinforce these joints with glue blocks from underneath. I glue and screw the riser rippings to the back of the joint between the tops of the risers and the treads (see the bottom photo at left). I leave at least 1 in. between the ripping and the mitered stringer; I'll need this space for other glue blocks. I angle 1⅝-in. screws slightly forward through the ripping into the tread to pull the ripping to the riser.

I spread lots of glue on the two legs and the faces of the triangular blocks cut from the notches, fastening them to the mitered stringer with 1⅝-in. screws through the predrilled holes. They must make full contact with the tread and riser. Because the block is cut at about 45° to the direction of the grain, two gluing rules are fuzzy. The conventions are that glue doesn't hold well on end grain and that gluing wood with its grain perpendicular will cause one or both pieces to split. But this isn't quite end grain, so glue sticks. And they aren't really cross-grain glue joints, so the treads and risers don't crack.

Scotia molding hides gaps. The author nails the scotia to the stringer and tread with 1¼-in. nails. They're too short to come through the top of the tread.

Correct installation matters. Because the stair's notches weaken the mitered stringer, the author frames a wall to support the stair as part of the stair installation. Blocking behind the wall stringer guarantees adequate nailing for the moldings when the stairs are trimmed.

The last step in construction is cutting the cove molding, or scotia, for under the nosings and nailing it in place (see the right photo on p. 69). I square the ends of the return pieces, then make a 30° cut from the scotia's bottom to the top of its cove. This leaves the flat at the top of the scotia to continue around and mimic a mitered return.

They Had Better Fit

Setting the stairs is simple. I like to have at least three helpers and arrange them so that one person is up and three are down. If the stair is going over another well, such as for basement stairs, I cover the hole with planks so that no one falls in.

After lifting the stairs into place, I shim the housed stringer away from the studs (usually with ½-in. plywood) to allow drywall to slide behind it. I shim the bottom so that finish flooring can slide snugly underneath. From below, I nail through the housed stringer and shims into the studs with 16d common nails. It's now safe to walk on the housed-stringer side of the stairs, but I think it's safer to stay off the mitered stringer until I build a wall under it (see the photo at left).

I usually frame this wall from 2x4s on the flat, shimmed away from the stringer for drywall. I nail the first stud in place in the middle of the stair. Then I have a helper stand on the mitered stringer to prevent it from being wedged upward as I install the rest of the studs.

Finally, I walk up and down the stairs to be certain they work. That's it. Absolutely no sorcery or expensive machinery involved.

Andy Engel is an executive editor at Fine Homebuilding *magazine and a former stairbuilder.*

Building an Exterior Newel Post

■ BY PETER CARLSON

I could hardly believe my good fortune when I landed a job at Preservation Park. This development in Oakland, California, is a collection of historically significant houses that were rescued from the wrecking ball. The dozen or so houses that make up the project were neglected, run-down, and in the way of other projects. But instead of carting them off to the landfill, the local redevelopment agency had the foresight to move the houses to a new neighborhood where they could be rebuilt into offices that honor Oakland's diverse architectural heritage.

The houses, which ranged in style from Tudor to Victorian, needed rebuilding. I was to rebuild the porches and the stairs, which had been lost during the moves. The newel posts I built for Trobridge House (see the photo on p. 72) are good examples of the work I did at Preservation Park. And while Trobridge House is a Victorian of the Italianate style, the methods I used to build the newels certainly could be adapted to other styles.

Custom-Milled Moldings

The Italianate style enjoyed the height of its popularity in the 1870s. The style drew heavily on massive, classical masonry motifs for inspiration, translated into wood by the ingenious millworking machines of the Industrial Revolution. The ubiquity of mills made highly finished materials readily available to the contractor for jobs both big and small.

Long gone is the vast selection of off-the-shelf Victorian house parts. But here in the San Francisco Bay area, there are still a few mills that can duplicate the old trim. Guided by bits of paint-encrusted molding from Trobridge House, the venerable El Cerrito Mill and Lumberyard in the nearby town of the same name ground shaper knives to mill crown, base, panel moldings, and handrails for this job (see the left drawings on p. 73).

line of the handrail with the prongs helping to stabilize the newel from the side. The steel post base requires careful layout because the location of the newel must be decided before the concrete is placed.

Start by Drawing

The newel and the handrail are among the most visible of finish details, and the materials to make them are often complicated and expensive. Even if the working drawings look to be accurate and complete, I do a full-size elevation and section drawing of a newel post before I start cutting materials. In their reduced size, working drawings have a way of obscuring problems that show up at full scale.

The newel is square in plan and has panels framed by panel moldings, rails, and stiles (the horizontal and vertical members, respectively, of a frame). The heart of the newel is a simple box, the sides of which ultimately become the faces of the panels. The dimensions of the panels govern all other parts, so I began by drawing them, which determined the size of the box. Once I made my drawing, I could take direct measurements for all the parts.

The elevation drawing also allows me to study the intersection of the rail with the newel. With it I can determine the post height, the angle of the handrail intersection and the true proportion of panels, crown, and other trim. Superintendents often balk at the time I spend making these drawings. I remind them of the old chestnut, "The only time thinking is seen is when it is not there."

Italianate Victorian stair. Massive shapes inspired by classical stonework distinguish the Italianate style. The newel posts, which support the handrail at the first tread, conceal pressure-treated posts anchored to the concrete landing. Because the house is now a commercial office, auxiliary handrails were required to meet contemporary codes.

As the primary anchorage for the handrail, the newel post must be firmly connected to the landing.

Tied to the Ground

As the primary anchorage for the handrail, the newel post must be firmly connected to the landing. The most typical method (and the one used on this job) is to build the newel around a pressure-treated post that is bolted to a steel post base. Set in concrete, the base keeps the bottom of the post from getting wet by elevating it slightly above the ground. As shown in the right drawing on the facing page, the base should be oriented so that the bolts are perpendicular to the

A Built-Up Newel Post

A pressure-treated 4x4 post affixed to a steel post base lies at the core of this Victorian newel. It is wrapped with furring to bring it out to the required profile for a proper Italianate newel post. The finish layers begin with the panels, followed by rails and stiles, panel moldings, and finally, the two-part base that wraps the bottom of the newel. A cap supported by crown molding finishes off the top.

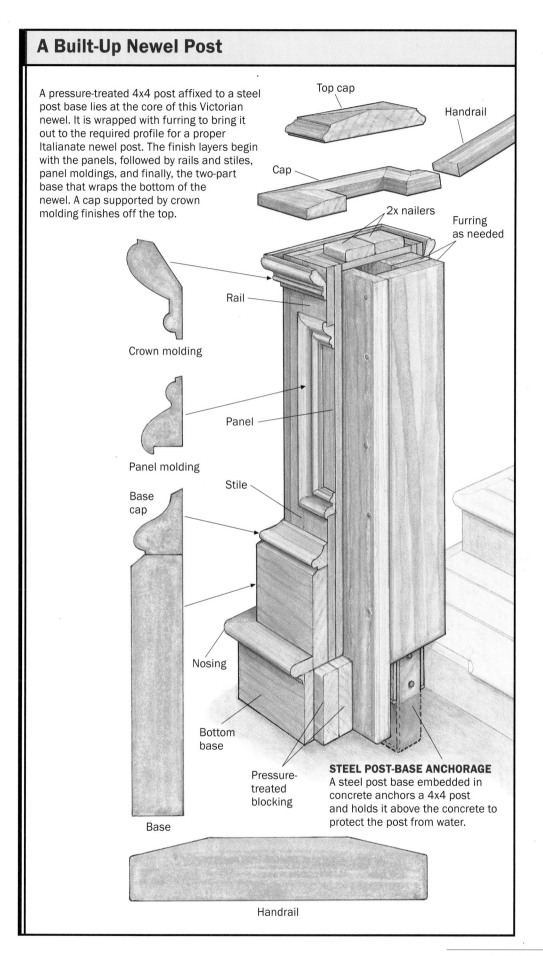

Top cap

Handrail

Cap

2x nailers

Furring as needed

Rail

Crown molding

Panel

Panel molding

Base cap

Stile

Nosing

Bottom base

Base

Pressure-treated blocking

STEEL POST-BASE ANCHORAGE
A steel post base embedded in concrete anchors a 4x4 post and holds it above the concrete to protect the post from water.

Handrail

Decorating
the Basic Box

I assemble the box around squares of solid
wood or plywood (see the left photo below).
Typically the lower square is left loose and
used only for layout, and the top is permanently installed as backing for the trim
pieces that cap the newel.

The stiles are affixed to the corners of the
box core—like corner boards on a clapboard-
sided house. They are long and narrow and
run the full height of the newel. To develop a
solid corner, I avoid miters—they always
open up over time when they're outdoors.
Accordingly, one stile must be ¾ in. (the
thickness of the material) smaller than its

Clamp, then nail. Rails and stiles are held in
position by pipe clamps while they are nailed.
The rails should be about ¹⁄₃₂ in. long to ensure
no gaps between the rails and the stiles.

Start with a box. A simple box is the core of
this multilayered newel post. A piece of solid
wood at the end helps keep the pieces square
during assembly. Here the author aligns a
stile assembly before nailing it to the box.

The trim carpenter's friend. The rabbeted
edge of a panel molding allows the trim
pieces to be loose-fitting while concealing
any gaps between the trim and the frame.

Base wrap. A mitered 2x frame forms the base of the newel post. Before attaching the frame to the newel, the author used a block plane to knock down any high spots at the butt joints between rails and stiles.

Stiles   Rail   Panel   Base

mate to maintain symmetry. Here's a simple way to rip both pieces with just one table-saw setting: Set the fence and rip the wider stile, then place a piece of the stock you are using against the fence when you cut the second board. This will quickly and accurately give you the setting for the narrower stile.

Before attaching them to the box, I pre-assemble the pairs of stiles, using nails and an exterior-grade glue. I use Titebond® II, the waterproof yellow glue. I think it's adequate given the fact that the surfaces will be painted. When I start nailing the pieces to the box, I'm careful to place fasteners, wherever possible, in spots that will be concealed by subsequent layers of trim. And if the design calls for edge routing, I keep fasteners out of the line of the router's cut.

By the way, I've become a believer in back-priming (even though the superintendent claims we're doing the painter's job). Before I attach the various layers of material to the boxes, I squirt their backsides with a water-based acrylic sealer. This step helps keep the tannins in the redwood from leaching into the final paint job and minimizes swelling and shrinking that result from changing weather conditions.

I cut the rails about $\frac{1}{32}$ in. long to make sure that the assembled frames weren't held apart by the underlying box (see the top right photo on the facing page). Once I had the rails and the stiles affixed to the boxes, I applied the panel molding. A true panel mold is designed to be the carpenter's friend. Along one edge it has a narrow rabbet the depth of the stiles and the rails. The lip of the rabbet covers the perimeter of the panel (see the bottom right photo on the facing page). The rabbet allows the carpenter to fashion accurate miters quickly by slightly undersizing the molding. The rabbet lip hides gaps between the molding and the rails or stiles. You just cut the pieces to fit a little loosely, assemble them into a picture frame, pop the frame into place and nail it.

I attached the top half of the baseboards next (see the photo at left). On the finished newel, the nosing of the bottom tread wraps around the newel (see the photo on p. 72), becoming a design element in its own right. I installed the nosing and the bottom half of the base after the newels were installed. That way I could scribe the bottom base to fit the concrete landing.

Installing Post and Cap

I added pressure-treated furring to the post for solid backing (see the photo at right). Each furring piece engages the concrete or the first tread, adding stability to the assembly. I left about ¼-in. gap between the furring and the inside of the box to allow for adjustment.

Fur out the post. Pressure-treated lumber nailed to the post stabilizes the newel and provides backing for the newel. The 2x nailers atop the newel are for attaching the cap.

Headed home. The author slips the nearly completed newel over the built-up post. The post is about ¼ in. smaller than the inside of the newel, which allows some room for adjustment.

Then I slid the newel over the post (see the photo at left). If the layout of the post base is off, you can make final adjustments at this point so that the newel will be plumb and square to the handrail. The post was shimmed solid and fastened with 3-in. long galvanized screws placed where they would be concealed by layers of trim (see the left photo on the facing page).

There are two basic designs for newel caps used on the houses in Preservation Park: unconnected handrail and connected handrail. The first is the easy one because the handrail simply dies into the side of the newel below the cap. The cap protects the interior of the newel. In addition to protecting the newel's interior, the second cap design has to include a mitered transition for the handrail (see the top right photo on the facing page).

In the heyday of Victorian construction in Oakland, the simple cap seems to have been more common. I've found that working drawings for restoration projects often complicate the originals. This job, of course, called for the more complicated of the two. My full-size drawings were invaluable in figuring out the angle of the miter required to meet the rail.

I made the cap from pieces of the redwood handrail that I ripped in half. The miters around the newel cap get all the weather, so they must be crafted carefully. The stock should be kept dry and allowed to acclimate before assembly. I back primed each piece, used plenty of glue in the joints, and cross-nailed them with pneumatic fasteners. I bedded the cap in a layer of caulk around the perimeter of the newel.

Screwed down tight. Trios of 3-in. long galvanized screws secure the newel to the post at top and bottom. The screws are driven in places where they will be concealed with trim.

Double-duty cap. Most newel caps simply keep the weather out of the newel. This one, however, includes a beveled piece of handrail for intersecting the handrail of the balustrade.

Sources

Ulmia
(Distrib. by)
Robert Larson
3450 Third St., 3B
San Francisco, CA
94124
(800) 356-2195
www.rlarson.com

A frame of crown molding supports the bottoms of the cap pieces (see the photo at right). Like the rails, I cut the crown pieces a bit long to avoid fussing over the joints. I tacked finishing nails to the rails and the bottom of the cap to hold the crown moldings as I tested them for fit. For this kind of dry fitting, miter clamps are very useful. I use the West German ones made by Ulmia. Once I dry-fit the crown moldings, I fasten them with the pneumatic fasteners. The clamps are equally indispensable for the base cap.

A top cap made from a single piece of stock completes the top of this newel. Because it has some end grain exposed to the weather, I applied several coats of primer to it before bedding the top cap in a thick bead of caulk.

Peter Carlson lives in Oakland, CA, and is a carpenter and member of Carpenters Union Local 713.

Clamping crown. A band of crown molding flares out the base of the cap while supporting it. Here the author dry-fits the pieces using miter clamps to hold the corners together.

Installing Stair Skirtboards

■ BY BOB SYVANEN

I used to trim closed-stringer stairways by installing 1x10 skirtboards first and butting the treads and risers into them. Setting the first riser was simple enough—scribe, cut, and nail in place. The difficulty started with the first tread. If it was the least bit long, it pushed the skirtboard, opening the joint below between the riser and the skirt. Installing the second riser then risked opening the joint at the first tread, and so on up the stairway.

A few years ago a young carpenter showed me a technique that involves notching the skirtboard for the treads and risers (it looks like an upside-down carriage). This method still requires scribe-fitting the treads, but eliminates scribe-fitting the risers because they slip behind the skirtboard. It produces a better-looking job quicker and with less aggravation.

Positioning the Skirtboards

As an example, let's consider a straight-run stairway with walls on both sides. I install the outside carriages 3 in. in from the finished walls. This leaves access for work that must be done from the backside. Also, the underside of the stairway should be open (no drywall) for nailing and gluing access.

I lay a 1x10 skirtboard against a wall so that the bottom can be scribed to fit the floor (see the drawing on the facing page). If the carriage was against the wall, then I could rest the skirtboard on the carriage points. But I have to jockey the skirt a bit to make sure it's parallel to the carriage. With its bottom corner resting on the first floor and its upper edge resting on the second floor, I move the 1x10 up or down until the angle looks right. I check it by measuring the distance from the points on the carriage to the upper edge of the 1x10.

I tack the 1x10 in place and mark the wall along the upper edge of the board—one mark near the top and one near the bottom. These serve as parallel reference marks for determining the skirtboard's final position.

While the 1x10 is tacked in place I scribe the bottom end to fit the floor. The simplest way to do this is to place a short length of 1x4 flat against the bottom end of the 1x10. The top edge of this piece will be parallel to the floor. Marking along this line will provide the angle at which to cut the skirtboard. Later I'll calculate exactly how much I need to trim.

After removing the 1x10, I return to the wall with the parallel reference marks and determine the top edge of where the skirt will eventually go. The skirtboard should sit as

Positioning the Skirtboard

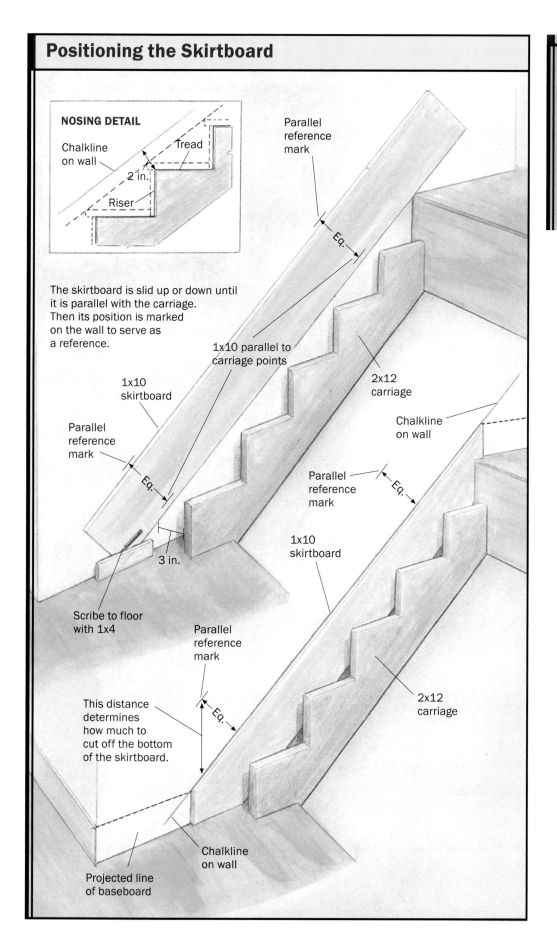

NOSING DETAIL

Chalkline on wall

Tread

2 in.

Riser

Parallel reference mark

The skirtboard is slid up or down until it is parallel with the carriage. Then its position is marked on the wall to serve as a reference.

1x10 parallel to carriage points

1x10 skirtboard

2x12 carriage

Parallel reference mark

Eq.

Chalkline on wall

Parallel reference mark

Eq.

1x10 skirtboard

Eq.

3 in.

Scribe to floor with 1x4

Parallel reference mark

This distance determines how much to cut off the bottom of the skirtboard.

Eq.

2x12 carriage

Projected line of baseboard

Chalkline on wall

The skirtboard should sit as high as possible without exposing any wall where the riser and tread meet.

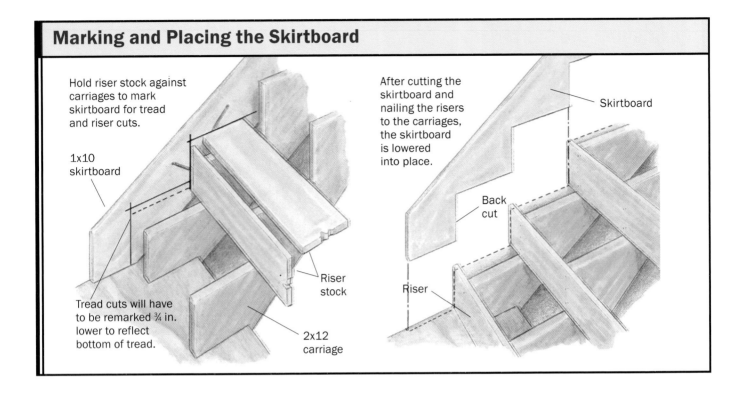

Hold riser stock against carriages to mark skirtboard for tread and riser cuts.

1x10 skirtboard

Tread cuts will have to be remarked ¾ in. lower to reflect bottom of tread.

Riser stock

2x12 carriage

After cutting the skirtboard and nailing the risers to the carriages, the skirtboard is lowered into place.

Skirtboard

Back cut

Riser

high as possible without exposing any wall where the riser and tread meet. The top edge of the skirtboard usually ends up about 2 in. beyond the finished tread nosing (see the detail on p. 79). I snap a chalkline on the wall representing the upper edge of the skirtboard; I then use a level to draw the plumb cut at the top and bottom of the wall, where the baseboard will meet the skirtboard. I also draw a plumb line through one of the parallel reference marks and then measure along it between the reference mark and the chalkline. This distance determines how much I need to cut off the bottom of the skirtboard.

If I'm using 1x stock for baseboard, I'll extend the skirt as far as necessary to intersect it. Next I transfer the layout of the plumb cuts to the skirtboard. To do this I measure the height of the plumb line on the wall and use an adjustable bevel square for the angle. Then I find the point on the skirtboard where I can get the height I need at the angle.

I follow the same procedures for both skirtboards, make the necessary cuts, and then tack them in place. At this point the skirtboard is between the wall and the carriage, and I'm ready to mark the cuts for treads and risers.

Marking and Cutting

To locate the riser cuts, I use a length of riser stock, cut square at the ends, and press it up against the riser surface of the carriages and hard against the skirtboard (see the drawing on the facing page). I mark the location of each riser on the skirtboard with a sharp pencil. I do the same for the treads, still using the riser stock, marking horizontal tread lines. These tread lines, however, have to be re-marked ¾ in. lower to represent the bottom face of the treads (or the horizontal surfaces of the carriage). I re-mark them later.

You can use a circular saw to cut the skirtboards, but I prefer to cut them by hand. A sharp finish handsaw is best for the riser cuts. I back-cut them (cut them at a slight angle) for a good, tight joint at the face. The tread cut will be hidden so I use an 8-point crosscut saw here.

Running the Risers

I like to rip all the risers to width before assembly. I keep the risers a hair narrower than called for and a bit short in length for a loose fit between the finished walls on each

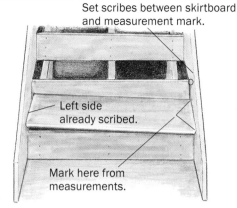

Set scribes between skirtboard and measurement mark.

Left side already scribed.

Mark here from measurements.

1. With tread ripped to width and cut ¾ in. long scribes are set at ⅜ in. to mark left side.

2. After scribing and cutting left side, measurements are taken to determine length of tread. Measure back and front with folding extension rule.

3. Right side is scribed to fit contours of skirtboard and marked for length at the same time.

side of the stairway. I rip the treads to allow for a 1-in. nosing and crosscut them about ¾ in. longer than the dimension between the skirtboards. This allows me to slip them into position at a low enough angle to get a good scribe at one end while leaving enough stock to scribe and cut the other end.

When nailing the risers in place, I hold the top edge flush with the tread surface of the carriages. After all the risers are in, I'll nail the skirtboards in place, but before doing that I locate the studs and blocking behind the drywall and mark the locations on the wall just above the chalkline that represents the top edge of the skirtboard. If there's a lack of solid blocking, I nail where I can and glue elsewhere with construction adhesive. Sticks wedged over to the opposite wall will secure the skirtboards firmly until the adhesive sets.

No matter how carefully the skirtboards are marked and cut, some joints will open where they butt against the risers. This is easily fixed by driving shims between the riser and the carriage, and then nailing with 5d box nails through the back of the riser into the skirtboard. I do this nailing after all the risers are in.

Scribing the Treads

Next the treads are scribed to the skirtboards on each end. Having allowed ¾ in. for scribing when I cut the treads to length, I set the scribes at ⅜ in. I put the tread in place with the end to be scribed down on the carriage and against the skirtboard (see the drawing above). The other end will ride high on the opposite skirtboard. The tread must be snug to the riser along the entire length. With the scribes riding against the skirtboard, I mark a line on the tread.

I back-cut the tread using a finish handsaw, but keep the cut square at the front where the nosing projects. Back-cutting makes it easier to correct the cut with a block plane.

After the first end is fitted, I carefully measure the distance between the skirtboards, using a folding rule with a sliding extension. I measure the length of both the front and back of the tread as a double-check. With the tread in place, the scribes should be set to one of the marks, and then should hit the other. If the scribe misses the second mark, it means the tread is tipped, and adjusting the tipping will ensure a good scribe line.

Bob Syvanen is a builder in Brewster, MA and a consulting editor for Fine Homebuilding.

Back-cutting makes it easier to correct the cut with a block plane.

Making a Bullnose Starting Step

■ BY STEPHEN WINCHESTER

Most trim carpenters are comfortable hanging doors and casing windows, but when it comes to stairs, they call in a specialist. Stairs really aren't that difficult to construct and install if you take a bit of care, don't rush, and make your joints as if the President himself were going to inspect your work.

On a recent job, I built a staircase with a double-bullnose starting step. The starting step is the first riser and tread on a stair. It's wider than the rest of the staircase and has curved ends, called bullnoses, that anchor the newel posts. In this article I'll explain how I made the starting step pictured here. Each staircase is different, so the dimensions I use here won't work for every stair, but the technique applies to any starting step.

Start with the Tread

I have a small shop where I make the treads, risers, and moldings, but these components could also be made on site. I don't have a lathe, however, so I buy manufactured newels and balusters rather than make them. I also buy handrails and fittings. The stairs themselves, on the other hand, I usually frame on site, which is what I did on this project.

After installing the mitered finish stringers (the trim boards on the sides of the stairs) over the rough stringers and drywall, I measured the finished width of the staircase at the bottom step. On the starting step this is the dimension between the curved ends of the riser. The width of this stair is 42½ in. The bullnoses extend about 14 in. beyond the finished stringers, so the overall length of the starting tread blank is 70½ in. But I don't cut the tread to the exact length yet.

If I have a wide enough piece, I make my tread blank from solid stock. Otherwise, I glue it up from narrower stock and match the grain so that the tread doesn't look like a zebra. Manufactured tread blanks will work, but they're often glued up from narrower stock, and the grain doesn't always match. For this stair the run, or tread depth, is 10½ in. I added 1⅛ in. for nosing on the front and another

The first step. An open stair—where the finished stringers aren't boxed in by the walls—makes it possible to have a double bullnose starting step. The riser is kerf-bent around forms that fit over the mitered stringers, and the tread is notched to fit in front of the second riser.

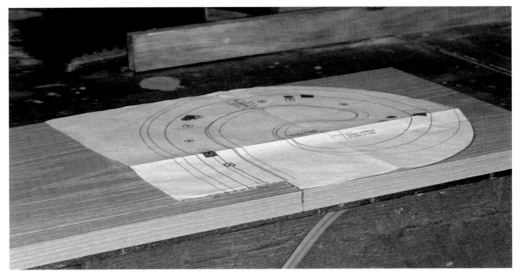

Forming the tread. A template is used as a pattern for cutting the bullnose ends on the tread. The cutout corner of the template aligns with the riser-skirt notch cut out of the tread.

1⅛ in. for nosing on the back of the tread where the bullnose ends curve around. So I needed 12¾-in.-wide stock. I use 1-in. thick stock for treads; ¾-in. stock is okay but looks a little flimsy.

To get 1⅛ in. nosing all around the starting tread, it's necessary to notch the back of the tread so that it fits over the second riser. The length of this notch equals the finished width of the stairs—42½ in.—and its depth equals the size of the nosing: 1⅛ in. When notched, the tread is 11⅝ in. deep where it hits the second riser and 12¾ in. deep only on the bullnose ends.

Cutting the Bullnose

On this staircase the newel posts are capped by a spiraling section of handrail called a volute. The manufacturer of the stair parts (L.J. Smith, Inc.) includes a paper template with the volute. The template helps you drill the starting step for the installation of the newel post and the balusters; I also

used it to determine the radius of the bullnose ends on my starting step.

I cut out the corner of the template for the second-riser notch so that I could position the template on the starting tread (see the photo above). Using the outline of the volute as a guide, I added ⅞ in. to the radius of the volute, then used a compass to trace a half-circle on the template to shape the bullnose. Then I cut the template along the half-circle I drew and traced the bullnose on each end of the tread blank.

To cut the bullnose ends, I used my bandsaw, but a jigsaw will work on site. I clamped the tread to the bench and belt-sanded the saw makes. Then I used a ⅜-in. roundover bit in the router on the top and bottom of the tread to shape the nosing. After sanding, the tread was complete.

You know you've got the proper spacing when the stock bends around the form easily.

Building the bending form. By scribing around the bullnose ends of the tread with a compass, the author determines the size and shape of the bending form. Each block is made from glued-up framing lumber; the blocks are placed on the tread and are held in place with a plywood spacer.

Making a Bending Form

Because I draw the shape of the riser on the tread, the tread becomes the pattern for the curved riser. I put the tread upside down on my workbench, set my compass to 1⅛ in. (the nosing dimension) and scribed around the edge of the tread. This mark created the shape of the riser that would support the tread. Because the riser stock is ¹³⁄₁₆ in., I scribed a second mark on the tread ¹³⁄₁₆ in. inside the first to create the inside dimension of the riser. I drew a line across the tread at each end of the second-riser notch to show where the mitered stringers butt against the tread.

Using the innermost mark, I measured the diameter and halved it to get the radius. Knowing the radius, I then made D-shaped bending forms for the curved riser out of kiln-dried framing lumber. Again, a bandsaw comes in handy for cutting the curved forms, but they could be cut with a jigsaw and belt-sanded smooth. I cut eight D-shaped blocks on the bandsaw and glued them together so that I had two stacks of four, each stack being 6 in. high. When the glue was dry, I trued up the curved edges on the bandsaw.

Next I set the glued-up blocks in place on the underside of the tread and screwed a plywood spacer to the blocks (see the photo above). I turned the form over and screwed a second piece of plywood to the other side.

Kerfing with a radial-arm saw. Kerfs are cross-cuts that don't cut completely through the stock. Here the kerfs are ⅜ in. o. c., and the face is ¹⁄₁₆ in. thick. Although the author used a radial-arm saw, a circular saw, a straightedge, and elbow grease will yield the same results.

Perfectly kerfed. Kerfing begins before the form bends to eliminate tension in the riser stock; well-kerfed wood wraps around the form like a piece of paper. Here the kerfed stock is temporarily clamped so that the other bullnose end can be marked for kerfing.

Hugging the curves. The riser is glued and clamped to the forms. Because the kerfed riser bends easily around the forms, the clamps are just snug enough to keep the stock in contact with the forms. Once the glue dries, the ends of the riser are trimmed to butt into the mitered stringers.

Kerfing the Riser

After selecting a piece of stock from the pile of stair lumber, I made some sample kerfs—crosscuts that don't go completely through the wood—on the radial-arm saw (see the top left photo on the facing page). When the kerfs are right, a riser will bend easily around a form, and the kerfs should just about close up on the inside of the bend. No heat or steam is necessary. My riser bend required that the ⅛-in.-wide kerfs be cut ⅜ in. o. c. and ¾ in. deep. The uncut face of the riser ended up about ¹⁄₁₆ in. thick.

I tried a couple of different spacings before I got it right. I usually start with kerfs ½ in. o. c., then check to see if the wood bends smoothly around the form. You know you've got the proper spacing when the stock bends around the form easily. Remember, different species will not bend the same way. In other words, don't make trial cuts in pine when bending a piece of oak.

To measure the length of the piece I needed, I wrapped my tape measure around the forms and added about a foot for safety. This riser stock was almost 10 ft. long. I kerfed one end of the riser, beginning about 1½ in. before the start of the curve so that the riser wouldn't kink as I bent it around the form. After clamping the kerfed end temporarily on the form (see the top right photo on the facing page), I marked the start of the second bend (plus 1½ in.) and cut those kerfs. A kerfed piece is pretty delicate and must be carefully handled.

Gluing and Clamping

I set the form on the upside-down tread and held them together temporarily with a few spring clamps. The glued-up blocks are part of the installed riser, so I coated them heavily with yellow glue and drizzled some into the riser kerfs, too. Clamping one end with a pair of bar clamps, I quickly but carefully bent the riser around the form and clamped the other end (see the bottom photo on the facing page). You don't need much pressure to hold the riser in place; that's why I didn't bother with clamping blocks.

I nailed the riser to the forms on what would be the back of the step. As soon as the riser was nailed to the forms, I took the riser off the tread. Otherwise, excess glue would have bonded the riser to the tread, and it wasn't time to put these two together yet. The next day, after the glue had set, I cranked my radial-arm saw way up to cut the extra length off the back of the riser. If you're doing it on site, use a circular saw and a square for this job. A 2° bevel on the cut ensures a tight fit to the finished stringers. The plywood spacers stay on until I am ready to install the riser.

Making Curved Scotia Molding

Scotia molding (or cove molding) is traditionally installed under the nosing of each tread on a stair. This molding hides the joint between tread and riser. To make the curved

Making Curved Scotia Molding

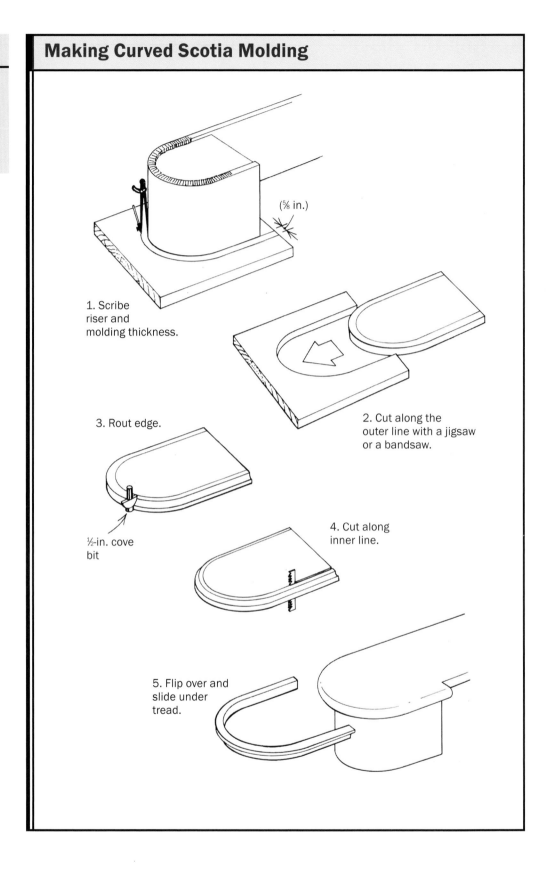

1. Scribe riser and molding thickness.

(⅝ in.)

2. Cut along the outer line with a jigsaw or a bandsaw.

3. Rout edge.

½-in. cove bit

4. Cut along inner line.

5. Flip over and slide under tread.

It fits. Careful measuring and cutting pay off when the completed riser slips over the mitered stringers. Construction adhesive and nails fasten the curved riser to the stringers; the tread is installed once the front of the riser is perfectly straight.

scotia for underneath the bullnose starting tread, I began by setting the riser upside down on a scrap of oak that was wide and long enough to make a U-shaped piece (see the drawing on p. 88). First I traced around the riser and then set my compass to ⅜ in. and traced around again. This second line is the outside edge of the molding. I marked a piece for each end of the riser, cut the outside curve on the bandsaw and then ran a router around each piece. The scotia profile is shaped with a ½-in. cove bit in the router. Then I went back to the bandsaw and cut the inside line. An identification letter or number helps me remember on which end of the riser each piece of molding fits.

Installing the Step

After removing the plywood spacers from the riser, I set it in place to check that it fit against the finished stringers. I squeezed construction adhesive on the finished stringers and set the riser back in place (see the photo above). Then I drilled pilot holes and nailed the riser tight to the front of each rough stringer. I then held a straightedge to the face of the riser to make sure the riser was straight. (If it's not, a tap behind the low spot will make it straight. When the construction adhesive hardens, it fills the gap between the center stringer and the riser.) To pull the ends of the riser tight to the finished stringers, I ran a couple of screws through the inner faces of the rough stringers into the curved bending forms.

Installing a Starting Newel

■ BY BOB GOODFELLOW

A starting newel provides most of the support for a handrail at the bottom of a stairway. A 1½-in. dowel tenon, turned on the end of the newel post, anchors the starting newel to a starting step. Wedging this dowel below the subfloor is the best way I know to install a starting newel so that it won't loosen up.

When you order your starting newel, get one with a dowel about 14 in. long so that it will extend clear through the starting step and the subfloor with length to spare. But before you bore a 1½-in. hole through the starting step and the subfloor, go downstairs and make sure there are no pipes, heating ducts, or electrical wires in your path. Then begin work on the starting step. Establish the location of the 1½-in. hole on the starting tread by using the stair manufacturer's template. Pay careful attention to where you mark the hole because the starting newel's location directly influences the alignment of the handrail components.

If you drill carefully, the starting newel will sit plumb in the bore. If not, a little judicious reaming should rectify the situation. Make sure the tread is clean so that when you stick the dowel into the hole, the bottom of the newel is completely seated against the tread. Then go downstairs and mark the dowel where it penetrates the subfloor. Mark all the way around the dowel, then make a second mark to indicate the direction that the floor joists run.

The marks you made show you where to drill out a slot in the dowel for a wedge.

STARTING NEWEL INSTALLATION

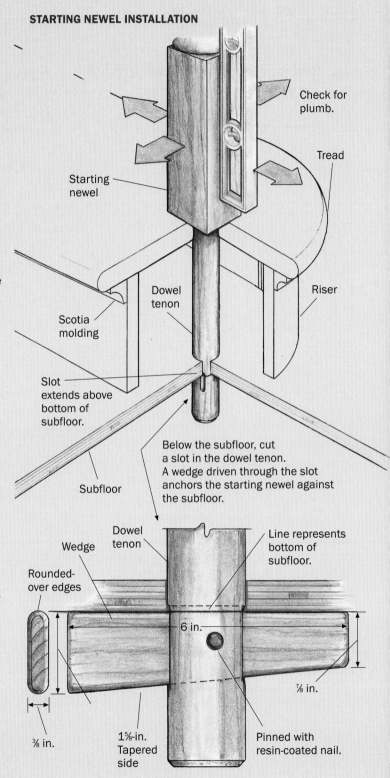

Check for plumb.

Tread

Starting newel

Dowel tenon

Riser

Scotia molding

Slot extends above bottom of subfloor.

Below the subfloor, cut a slot in the dowel tenon. A wedge driven through the slot anchors the starting newel against the subfloor.

Subfloor

Dowel tenon

Wedge

Line represents bottom of subfloor.

Rounded-over edges

6 in.

⅞ in.

⅜ in.

1⅝-in. Tapered side

Pinned with resin-coated nail.

The mark around the dowel locates the top of the slot, and the second mark shows you in which direction the slot should face (parallel to the joists). Make the slot by drilling a series of ⅜-in. holes. Drill the top hole a little above the subfloor mark on the dowel and then drill the others below until you've made a slot about 1½ in. long. Clean out the burrs of wood with a chisel and a rasp. Then mark the base of the newel to show which way the slot faces.

I make the wedge that anchors the newel from a piece of ⅜-in. oak stock. The wedge, which is about 6 in. long, has a taper on one side only; the other side I leave square. The back end of the wedge should be about 1⅛ in. high, the front end about ⅞ in. high.

I also round over all the square edges; this way the wedge will have more contact with the slot in the dowel. Rounding over is done quickly with a block plane.

With the newel rotated according to the mark you made on its base, insert the dowel into the starting step. Then go downstairs with the wedge and your glue. Smear the wedge and the slot in the dowel with glue, then gently drive the wedge into the slot. It's a very good idea to have someone upstairs to yell, "OK!" when the newel is plumb and level. Don't bash the wedge in; you'll know when it's tight because it'll have a certain ring—dong, dong, ding—ah, that's it. Finally, drill a pilot hole and use a resin-coated nail to pin the wedge in place.

Bob Goodfellow is Creative Director at The Taunton Press, Inc.

Next, I set the tread into beads of construction adhesive squeezed onto the tops of the rough stringers, the top edge of the curved riser, and the bottom face of the second riser. I predrilled and nailed through the tread into the stringers with 10d finishing nails. Then I nailed the tread to the curved riser with 8d finishers. A couple of 6d box nails through the back of the second riser into the starting tread, along with plenty of construction adhesive, prevents a squeaky starting step. I don't use a nail gun to assemble the skirts, the risers, and the treads because I could miss what I'm trying to nail into, or a nail could veer off and shoot through the face of the work.

The scotia molding goes on next. The two U-shaped pieces go first, followed by a straight piece (which I also make) under the front of the tread connecting the two U-shaped pieces. I used a small brad gun to shoot the molding on. It's easier than handling small nails.

To anchor the newel posts, I drilled a 1½-in.-dia. hole in each end of the starting step, using the volute template to locate the holes. I drilled through the tread and the 2x bending forms. Then I cut the dowel tenons on the ends of the newel posts to length, coated them with construction adhesive and drove them into the holes until the base of the newels seated against the tread (see the sidebar at left)

Stephen Winchester is a carpenter and woodworker in Gilmanton, NH.

Making a Curved Handrail

■ BY JOHN GRIFFIN

As an apprentice carpenter, I admired the grace of curved handrails and marveled at the skill necessary to create them. How the stairbuilder bent oak into a rail of the correct shape and floated it so precisely above the stairs that the balusters and newels were plumb and regularly spaced seemed beyond any skills that I might hope to acquire.

Then came the day when two railing installers showed up at a house I was trimming. The skinny, adolescent helper shuttled tools and materials from the van to the house while the boss strolled around chewing an unlit cigar. Three days later, they were gone, leaving behind a couple of soggy cigar butts and a gorgeous balustrade.

Simply seeing the bending rail stock took much of the awe out of curved stair rails. Imagine a standard handrail ripped into thin, flexible strips (see the inset photo on the facing page). Glued and clamped to forms set on the stair, the strips solidify into a rail that follows the stair's curve.

Baluster Position Determines the Centerline of the Rail

I buy bending rail from a local supplier, but Coffman and L.J. Smith, both nationally distributed stair-parts manufacturers, also make bending rail. The bending rail that I use comes in several profiles that match standard straight railing. Each lamination has a bead milled in one side and a groove milled in the other. Adjacent strips interlock to keep the laminations in line during glue up. Bending rail is available with varying numbers of laminations. The more laminations, the thinner and more flexible each layer is. So the tighter the stair's radius, the more laminations needed for the rail to bend without breaking. For a 5-ft. radius such as this stair has, I used a 2¼-in.-wide rail composed of six laminations. For radii down to 30 in., seven laminations will get a 2¼-in.-wide rail around the bend.

Store-bought bending rail. Beads and grooves align the laminations, while soft-wood molds protect the rail from the clamps during glue up.

L-shaped brackets clamped to the stair make up the bending form. Sandpaper stuck to the brackets' bottoms improves their grip. Plywood protects the treads.

Also included with most bending rails are bending molds. These softwood strips are milled with a negative of the railing's profile on their inside. Bending molds go outside the rail during glue up to protect the rail and to give the clamps purchase.

The first step in bending a rail is laying out the baluster locations. Traditionally, the face of the first baluster on each tread aligns with the face of the riser below. The sides of all balusters should line up with the face of the finished stringer. This step keeps the holes drilled in the stair to fasten the balusters solidly in the treads. I typically space the balusters on centers equal to half the tread depth at the baluster line.

After placing protective pieces of plywood on the treads, I clamp L-shaped brackets to the nosing overhangs (see the top photo at left). Once secured in place, these brackets make up the form to which I'll clamp the rail during glue up. I bent my brackets from ¼-in. by 2-in. steel bar stock, but they can also be made from wood. However they're made, they must be rigid enough to resist the tension of bending the rail.

Begin with a dress rehearsal. With the unglued laminations bundled, the crew sets the rail in place, choreographing their movements. The rail's center is marked to guide placement once glued, and the clamps are opened to fit the rail.

Once glue up begins, you have 15 minutes to clamp the rail. Rollers spread the glue, and helpers stack the glued-up laminations. Plastic shrink wrap will hold the laminations together.

To establish the correct curve, it's critical that the brackets be clamped to the tread tangent to the inside edge of the handrail's bending mold. This line is half the combined thickness of the rail and the bending mold from the baluster centerline.

With All the Brackets in Place, It's Time for Glue Up

I use Titebond® Supreme glue, which is said to be better for ring-porous woods such as oak. It has an open time of 12 minutes to 15 minutes, not long, so I like to have at least three helpers for this stage. Franklin makes other glues with longer working times that may be easier to use with bending rails. I haven't tried them because I know Supreme works well and because I hesitate to experiment on a job as involved as a bent rail.

I begin with a dry run (see the bottom left photo on the facing page). This step synchronizes everyone, and it allows me to make some index marks on the rail to position it at the top and bottom of the staircase. During glue up, I begin clamping in the stair's middle. Without these index marks, it's possible to end up with one end of the rail too short and the other end beyond the forms. If that happens, there is no convenient way to continue curving the rail, and you have a fine mess. When bent, the rail stock should extend about 6 in. beyond each end of the stair to allow for trimming.

During the dry run, I lay all the necessary clamps on the treads and open them up to the proper width so that they're ready to go once the glue is spread. After the dry run, I take the bending rail from the forms and lay it on sawhorses, bead side up, with the two outside laminations good side down (see the bottom right photo on the facing page). I pour the glue into a paint tray, and using small disposable rollers, I paint one side of all but the last outside lamination with glue. I use plenty of glue and don't worry about squeeze out; a glue-starved area spells disaster.

Then I stack the pieces—bending mold, laminations and bending mold—finally shrink-wrapping the stacked rail in several places. This step helps to hold the rail together while it's being carried to the stair and clamped.

With the glued-up rail on the stair, two people clamp it to the forms, starting from the middle, while another two pull and twist the ends of the rail into alignment (see the photo below). It's important to press the railing tightly to each tread as you clamp. The

When bent, the rail stock should extend about 6 in. beyond each end of the stair to allow for trimming.

Clamping proceeds from the middle to the ends. Clamps hold the rail to the forms and keep the rail's bottom flat to the tread nosings. The crew watches for voids and adds clamps as needed.

After 24 hours, the rail is unclamped from its forms. The rail is placed on horses for preliminary smoothing. Scraping and belt-sanding remove most of the glue squeeze out.

rail's bottom should make full contact with the tread nosings. If only one point on the rail touches the nosings, the rail is twisting, and the bottom of the rail won't be level when it's installed. Joining a twisted rail to fittings such as volutes or goosenecks is much harder.

I check for voids between the laminations both top and bottom, and add clamps wherever necessary.

After 24 hours' drying time, the rail can be unclamped. I move it back to the sawhorses (see the photo above) and remove most of the dried-glue squeeze out with a sharp scraper and 80-grit sandpaper in a belt sander. Final profile and joint sanding happen later, after the fittings are attached.

Support the Rail in Its Final Position to Find the Cuts for the Fittings

The stair rail on this project intersects a balcony rail at the top, so the height of the top newel was determined by the height of the balcony guardrail (36 in.). Just as it would have done with a straight rail, the balcony rail passes over the newel higher than the stair rail. A standard two-riser gooseneck makes up the difference. At the bottom, this stair had a bullnose step, so the rail begins with a volute.

Setting the starting newel for a curved rail is a bit different than for a straight rail, as is my approach to marking the volute and gooseneck fittings for their cuts. Unlike straight rail, where all cuts are square to the rail's side, cuts made to join curved rails and fittings are square to the radius's tangent. Because the rail parts curve in from the tangent, the cuts are made at a slight angle. A compound-angle cut on a helical-shaped rail is difficult to lay out exactly the first time, and some fussing is called for. Although I might simply lay a straight rail on the tread nosings to mark the fitting cuts, I temporarily suspend a curved rail in its final position to locate the newel and to find the correct cut angle for the fittings.

To suspend the rail, I leave at least three brackets on the stairs, one top, one bottom and one center. I clamp some scrap-wood posts, with the range of allowable handrail height marked on them, plumb to these brackets (see the photos on facing page). (Check local building codes for handrail height requirements in your area.) The bent rail is clamped to the posts in the middle of the rail-height range.

Because the curve of the glued-up handrail relaxes a bit after it's unclamped, I brace the posts plumb to keep the rail true. The rail will be clamped and unclamped several times for cutting and test-fitting. Once I've established the height, I affix hand screws to the temporary posts to support the rail at the correct height as it's removed and replaced.

I use square-bottom starting newels long enough to penetrate the bullnose step and reach the floor. Normally, I use the template provided with the volute. In this case, however, the starting step narrowed so that this template wouldn't work. To locate this starting newel, I set the volute on it temporarily. Then I rested the newel plumb on the starting step. This process placed the volute above the rail, and I lined up the volute on the rail by eye (see the photo on p. 99). When I got this right, I scribed the newel location to the tread and jigsawed the hole for the newel.

Temporary posts hold the rail in its correct position. The range of acceptable rail height is marked on the posts' top. Once the posts are plumb, hand screws act as ledgers to register the rail's height, allowing it to be removed and replaced as needed.

Using a bull's-eye level to check for level, I again set the volute atop the newel and the newel on the tread, but behind its hole. I rotate the volute so that its up-easing parallels the rail. With the rail and volute lined up, I can eyeball them from the side and mark where their tops and bottoms intersect (see the top left photo below). These marks establish the cut on the volute. I then cut the volute on a chopsaw (see the top right photo below). For another method of marking volutes, see the drawing on the facing page.

At this point, the newel is still too long and will need trimming for its final height. I set the newel temporarily in its hole, with the volute on top. By measuring the difference in height between the volute and the rail, I can now see if the newel requires trimming. Sometimes, I can adjust the rail height up or down to meet the volute fairly; other times, I must trim the newel's height. If raising the rail, I'm careful to check that the balusters I have are not now too short. Also, if I change the rail height here, I do so on the other posts as well to keep things uniform.

With the newel set, I again put the volute in place. Using a combination square, I trans-

SNEAKING UP ON A PERFECT CUT

Eyeballing where rail is tangent to volute. The author marks these points on the volute's top and bottom.

Steady help is critical. The volute is blocked up so that the tangent points align with the chopsaw blade.

Transferring the cut to the rail. With the volute set atop the newel, the cut angle is transferred to the rail.

The author plumbs the rail while his helper checks the fit. It can take several trimmings to get it perfect.

fer the cut angle from the volute to the rail (see the bottom left photo on the facing page). With a helper, I remove the rail to the chopsaw and make the cut. Then I return the cut rail to its place and check the joint's alignment (see the bottom right photo on the facing page). Odds are it's not perfect yet, and I'll mark the needed adjustments, disassemble the rail and recut. This way, I sneak up on a perfect fit a hair at a time.

Locating the starting newel. The volute is lined up on the rail by eye. With the newel plumb and with the volute eyed up, the newel location is then scribed to the tread.

Marking a Volute on the Bench

If you're not comfortable eyeballing the cuts on a $100 volute, as discussed in the text, here's an alternative. These techniques also work on goosenecks, but the positions of the pitch block are reversed.

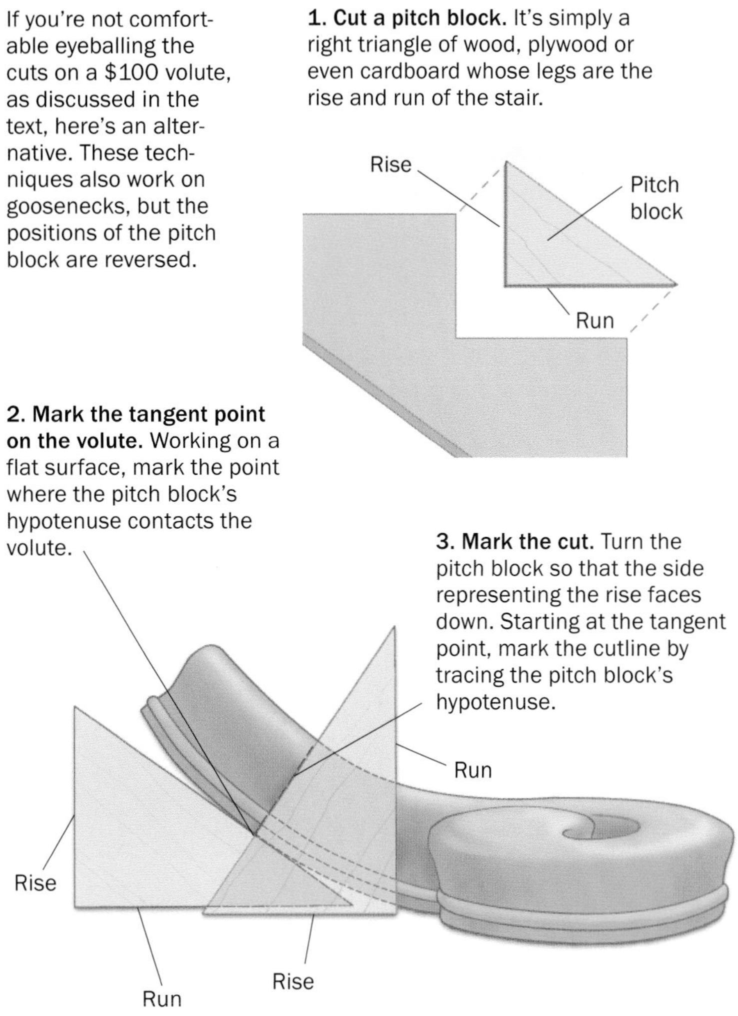

1. Cut a pitch block. It's simply a right triangle of wood, plywood or even cardboard whose legs are the rise and run of the stair.

Rise

Pitch block

Run

2. Mark the tangent point on the volute. Working on a flat surface, mark the point where the pitch block's hypotenuse contacts the volute.

3. Mark the cut. Turn the pitch block so that the side representing the rise faces down. Starting at the tangent point, mark the cutline by tracing the pitch block's hypotenuse.

Run

Rise

Run

Rise

Temporarily Assemble the Volute-to-Rail Joint

Once I've mated volute to rail, I take them down to drill them for rail bolts. I don't glue the joint yet, however, because it may be necessary to realign these components later. I install the gooseneck at the balcony newel the same way as the volute (see the photo below). Marking the cuts involves setting the horizontal surface of the gooseneck on the newel dead level while holding the up-easing (the curved portion) alongside the rail. Again, I like to sneak up on the cuts. Patience making these cuts beats replacing a miscut fitting.

The gooseneck at the balcony is marked much like the volute. With the author holding the fitting level, his helper marks the cut where the rail and fitting meet.

Once I'm sure the gooseneck fits as it should, I mark index lines across the joints and disassemble them. The joints are then glued and the rail bolts tightened. I also install all the plugs to cover the bolt holes in the bottom of the rail. Working with the rail on sawhorses, I smooth the joints in preparation for final installation.

When fastening this assembly to the newels, I coat the inside of the holes on the bottom of the fittings with glue rather than coating the dowel pins on top of the newels. This step keeps glue from smearing the bottom of the fittings or dripping down the newels. Once the rail is glued to the newels and reclamped to the center brace halfway up the stair, it's time to work on the balusters.

Double-Ended Lags Hold Balusters to Treads

Baluster installation is the same as with a straight rail. I plumb up from points marked on the treads, using an L.J. Smith Telescoping Baluster Marking Tool, and mark the rail. I used to drill holes in the treads to receive the pins on the balusters' bottoms. No more. I cut off the pins and drill a pilot hole in each baluster for a $\frac{5}{16}$-in. by $2\frac{1}{2}$-in. lag that's threaded on both ends (see the photo on the facing page). L.J. Smith also makes the Centaur Drill Guide, which quickly centers a drill over the bottom of standard-size balusters. Corresponding holes are drilled in the treads.

The holes drilled in the underside of the rail must be deep. This way, I can slide the untapered baluster tops far up into the rail so that the lags in their bottoms can swing into place over the hole in the tread. Once a baluster is threaded tight to the tread, I shoot a 1¼-in. brad through its top into the handrail to prevent any movement or rattling.

Final sanding and detailing are done with chisels and progressively finer grits of sandpaper. A professional finish requires running your hand up and down the handrail to check for flaws. As every finish carpenter knows, elbow grease and patience are absolute necessities if the finished product is to be a pleasure both to see and to feel.

John Griffin is a finish carpenter who works primarily in the Southwest.

Sources

Coffman
1000 Industrial Rd.
Marion, VA 24354
(276) 783-7251
www.coffmanstairs.com

Franklin International
2020 Bruck St.
Columbus, OH 43207
(800) 877-4583
www.franklin.com
Titebond Supreme

L.J. Smith
35280 Scio-Bowerston Rd.
Bowerston, OH 44695
(740) 269-2221
www.ljsmith.net

Double-ended lag joins baluster and tread. With the holes in the rail drilled extra deep, the author inserts the balusters, positions the lag over the tread and twists the baluster home. Pneumatic nails will secure balusters to the rails.

A Balustrade of Branches

■ BY DAN DAVIS

I had just finished building a conventional over-the-post balustrade with manufactured stair parts when Pete Giovali called. He, too, wanted a new staircase and handrail. But Pete has a taste for the unusual, and his new staircase and balustrade would be anything but out-of-the-catalog ordinary.

I planned to use traditional construction methods, but my source of materials for this balustrade was private forest land near Flagstaff, Arizona. I scoured stands of alligator juniper, which grows in gnarled, twisting forms, looking for branches that could be used for newels and balusters, and 90° bends for corners and easings. I also looked for long, straight, slim branches for the 8-ft., 10-ft., and 11-ft. rail sections. In the end, I milled the long rail pieces from Arizona cypress. Shorter rails on the staircase could be made from juniper. Once in the shop, I used a draw knife to peel the bark. A disk grinder did the heavy work, and I finished with a palm sander and sanding by hand.

To create a flat on the bottom of the balusters, I built a simple jig that held balusters plumb on my bench. Using a compass, I marked the bottom of each baluster and made the cut on a chopsaw. I then drilled a ½-in. hole for a dowel that would anchor it to the floor (see the photo below). At the top of each baluster, I used a tenon cutter. Because these balusters have no straight or square surfaces, they were

Keeping dowel holes straight. The author drills a ½-in. dowel hole in the bottom of a baluster. An inclinometer helps to keep the hole perpendicular.

Round tenons on crooked stock. An adjustable jig for the drill press holds a baluster top in position. Shoulders are trimmed with a handsaw.

Okay, everybody line up. String holds the balusters in place temporarily, allowing the author to check the spacing before drilling the rails.

difficult to hold in the drill press. An adjustable jig helped to stabilize the pieces (see the left photo above).

Fitting Pieces Requires Patience, Persistence, and Time

I imagined the dwarves' staircase in the Disney® movie *Snow White and the Seven Dwarfs,* with a dreamy look of newels growing through balconies. To create it, I had to invent some techniques and devote plenty of time—in all, the stair project took 1,500 hours, although not all of that was devoted to the balustrade.

With the new oak staircase built, the newel posts were the first pieces of the balustrade to go in. They all had to be scribed to fit. I held each piece in place for marking with straps clamped to the nosings and the bottom end resting on a ladder or a sawhorse. I wanted the nosings to die into the newels, but getting this fit exact was difficult. I scribed cutlines into the newel, then used a small chainsaw to make the rough

Drilling the rails for balusters. A Forstner bit makes a clean hole in the underside of the rail to accept the end of a baluster.

cuts. A disk grinder and chisels cleaned up the cuts, and I fine-tuned the joints with files, chisels, and a Dremel® tool. I left newels long, to be cut later to the height set by the assembled handrail. Newels are lagged in place through 1-in. holes that were later plugged.

With newels bolted temporarily in place, I chose the balusters and established their spacing, holding them in place temporarily with nylon line (see the top right photo on the facing page). When they looked right, I numbered the pieces, took them down and made the rails (see the bottom photo on the facing page). The curving starter rail was tricky to cut and fit (see the photo at right), but a sandbag on the table of the miter saw helped to keep oddly shaped pieces situated correctly and safely. The handrail is sanded to 220 grit (balusters to 120) and finished with tung oil.

Dan Davis is a stairbuilder and carpenter in Flagstaff, AZ.

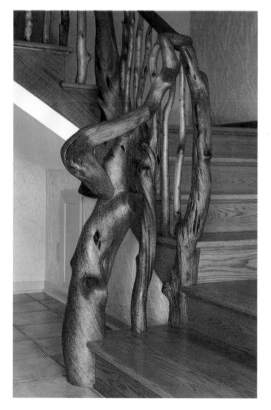

Months in the making. The author collected much of the raw material for this cypress and juniper balustrade from a forest, then painstakingly pieced it together for a client who was in the mood for something unusual.

A Freestanding Spiral Stair

■ BY STEVEN M. WHITE

As a woodworker, I have always liked curved staircases because they combine function with graceful, sculptural beauty. A spiral stair built around a central column is the simplest version of a curved staircase, but it's still a challenge to build. In this article I'll talk about a spiral stair that I've built for several clients and the straightforward techniques I've developed for fabricating its parts with common shop tools. For the twists involved in laying out a spiral stair, see the sidebar on p. 113.

Lightening the Visual Load

To my eye, most pole-supported spiral stairs are aesthetically flawed because they lack a graceful balustrade. Their handrails and balusters are often used as part of the structural support of the stair, and as a result they can look pretty clunky. To avoid this problem, my stair transfers the loads from the treads by way of cantilevered ribs that pass through a hollow column. This allows me to border the stair with a delicate row of balusters supporting a sinewy handrail.

Each tread/rib assembly resists three forces: the downward load of a person; twisting due to offset loading on the tread (the fact that a person would step near the front of a tread rather than directly over the rib); and horizontal, or back-and-forth, wiggle.

To resist the downward load, I use a strong, cantilevered rib that passes completely through the column and out the opposite side. Such a design transfers the load from the tread to purely vertical reactions on the column. It also allows the ribs to be revealed as tenons on the side opposite the treads. I put ½-in. chamfers on these tenons, emphasizing their sculptural qualities as they spiral from floor to floor.

For a 36-in. radius stair, I've found that a 2-in. by 6½-in. rib is adequately strong. Because the stresses on a cantilevered beam decrease with distance from the point of cantilever, I taper the ribs for the sake of appearance (see the drawing on p. 110).

I also know that a 2-in. by 6½-in. rib will sufficiently resist twisting at its outer end, and that treads made from solid 2x lumber will be strong enough to withstand the offset

Cantilevered treads. The author's spiral staircase rises on treads mounted atop ribs that extend through a hollow column. The treads wind their way from an enlarged first tread to a second-level landing that is borne primarily by ledgers affixed to the wall.

load. To minimize horizontal wiggle, I rely primarily on the tread itself being drawn tightly against the column with lag screws. In addition, I run the front baluster of each tread through the tread and into the tread below. This interlocks all the treads and further reduces any wiggle.

For this stair, I used vertical-grain Douglas fir throughout, which is a strong, attractive, and economical wood. Incidentally, I bought unsurfaced stock for the ribs because it's a full 2 in. thick. Then I dressed it myself, netting ribs 1¹³⁄₁₆ in. thick.

Cylindrical Column

The center column is round, with 24 mortises (two for each rib) in a precise spiral. To effect this, I build a 14-sided coopered cylinder in which the width of each stave is the same width as a rib.

First I ripped 9-ft. lengths of 2x6s into 1¹³⁄₁₆-in. wide staves, beveled inward at 12.86° on both edges. I got that number by dividing 14 into 360° and then dividing the result by 2. I fine-tuned the bevel by first running some scrap lumber and crosscutting it into 14 sections to see how they fit together. To ensure correct alignment of all the staves during assembly, I cut a ¼-in. wide groove down the center of each beveled edge for plywood splines.

The next step was laying out and cutting the rib mortises. I placed all the staves side by side on a large, flat surface and numbered them to avoid any confusion later. On each stave I marked a 6½-in. high mortise for the front side of one rib and a 3-in. high mortise for the protruding tenon of another rib. These mortise locations were laid out sequentially, at 8.156-in. intervals, corresponding to the rise of the stair (see the left photo below). I then crosscut each mortise

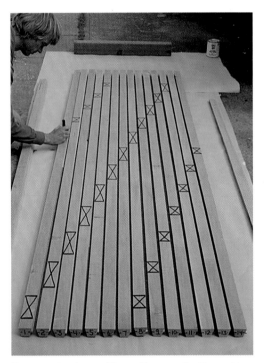

Coopered column. The author marks the entry and exit mortises on the collated staves prior to precutting the mortises.

Just a pinch. To keep the staves intact during glue-up, White does not cut the mortises all the way through.

with a power miter saw, being sure to leave a little wood uncut on the backside to keep the stave in one piece (see the bottom right photo on the facing page).

Now I was ready to assemble the column. I began by gluing up trios of staves, using pipe clamps to hold them together. I left the alignment splines and glue out of the mortise regions to ease the cleanout still to come. Then I glued up the four subassemblies using twisted ropes as clamps (see the photo below). Fourteen staves at 1¹³⁄₁₆-in. width yielded a column diameter of about 8 in.

Once the glue had dried, it was a simple matter to split out the mortise waste with a chisel. The resulting holes, however, were narrower on the inside than on the outside because of the stave being beveled, so I pared out the sides of the mortises with a chisel. I used a test rib to check for a snug, smooth fit through each mortise.

Column glue-up. Subassemblies of glued-up staves are clamped together so that their bottoms are in alignment.

To round the column, I planed down the 14 corners by hand to create a 28-sided cylinder. Then I used my plane and sandpaper to work the assembly into a smooth cylinder.

Treads and Ribs

I began the tread part of the project with a cardboard template. Each tread is ¹⁄₁₄ of a circle, or 25.71° of arc, and my template started as a simple pie slice at this angle with a 36-in. radius. To this I added 1¾ in. of width to both the front and back edges, to give a generous nosing and to widen the narrow end of the tread. The narrow end of each tread is curved to match the column's face. The curved corners flare into a straight cut that allows the tread to be let into dadoes cut into the column (see the photo on p. 116).

I glued up pairs of 2x12s to get the wide stock required for wedge-shaped treads. Then I sawed out the treads on the diagonal, making sure that the front edge of each tread was parallel to the grain. A trammel-point jig on my bandsaw helped me to cut smooth outside arcs on the treads.

All the treads are identical except for the starting tread and the landing tread (see the drawing on p. 111). Traditional staircases usually feature a prominent starting step, so I widened the first tread toward the newel post. I also widened the top landing to meet the door opening. The landing is flush with the second-story subfloor so that it can be carpeted to match the upstairs-hall floor.

I used a ¾-in. roundover bit to soften the edges of the ribs and treads. After a good sanding, I glued and screwed each tread to its rib. Each rib is under the centerline of its tread.

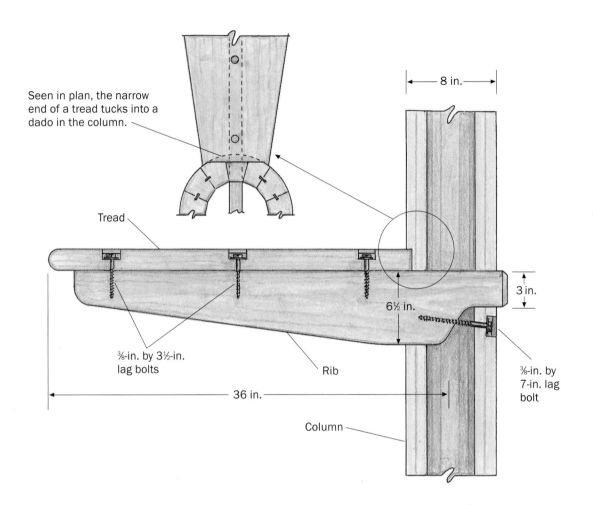

Seen in plan, the narrow end of a tread tucks into a dado in the column.

Tread

⅜-in. by 3½-in. lag bolts

Rib

8 in.

3 in.

6½ in.

⅜-in. by 7-in. lag bolt

36 in.

Column

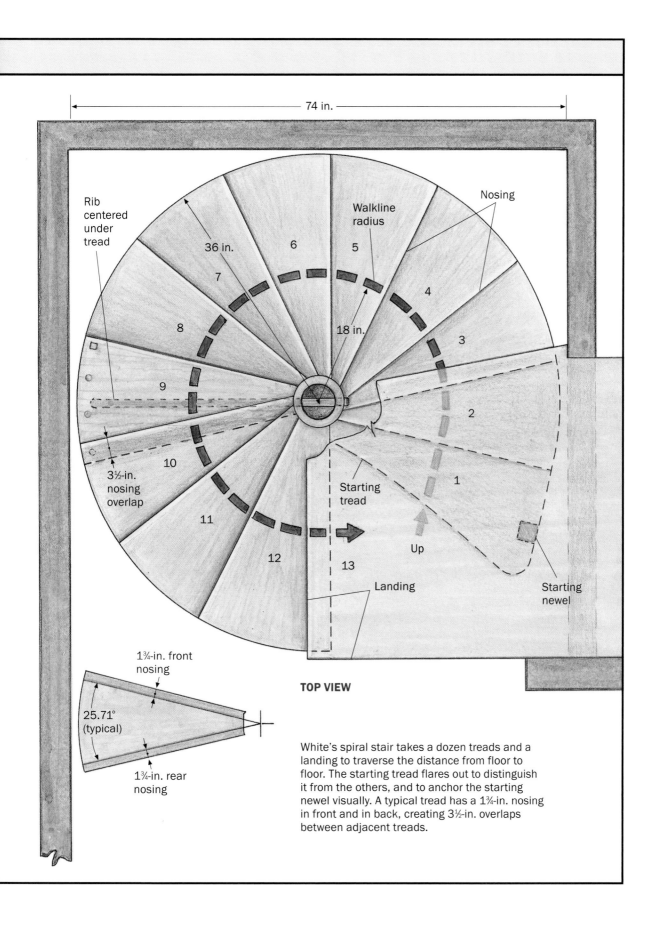

74 in.

Rib
centered
under
tree

Walkline
radius

Nosing

36 in.

6

5

7

4

18 in.

8

3

9

2

10

1

3½-in.
nosing
overlap

11

Starting
tread

12

13

Up

Landing

Starting
newel

1¾-in. front
nosing

TOP VIEW

25.71°
(typical)

1¾-in. rear
nosing

White's spiral stair takes a dozen treads and a
landing to traverse the distance from floor to
floor. The starting tread flares out to distinguish
it from the others, and to anchor the starting
newel visually. A typical tread has a 1¾-in. nosing
in front and in back, creating 3½-in. overlaps
between adjacent treads.

The Balustrade

I make spiral handrails by gluing up thin laminations over a bending form (see the photo below). This is a full-size cylinder representing the diameter and height of the staircase, and is made of spaced 2x4s screwed to plywood bulkheads laid on sawhorses. Because I was building an outer handrail, I built the cylinder to the exact radius of the inside of the handrailing, in this case 33⅛ in. I built the rail in two halves, so the form needed to be just half a cylinder, and only half the stair height—about 5 ft.

Calculating the angle at which the rail spirals up the cylinder is a straightforward rise/run calculation. In this case the unit rise was 8.156 in. and the unit run was ¼ the circumference of a 33⅛-in.-radius circle, or ¼ (2pi x r), which equals 14.87 in. Knowing the rise and run, the angle of ascent is $\tan^{-1}$ (rise/run) = 28.75°. With this information I plotted reference points on the 2x4s to guide the placement of the handrail laminations.

Starting with 10-ft.-long Douglas fir stock 2⅜ in. thick, I ripped nine laminations, each ¼ in. thick, for a 2¼-in. wide rail. Keeping the laminations in order makes for less-visible glue lines later. I use a ripping blade on my table saw and glue the sawn laminations unplaned.

For handrail laminations, I use a toothbrush to apply aliphatic resin glue. I then stack the laminations in order and carry them to the cylinder. I first clamp the center, then work outwards, clamping the rail to the 2x4s and aligning their edges with the reference points. Bending 2¼-in. worth of

Doing the twist. Stretched across a bending form made of 2x4s on plywood bulkheads that duplicate the radius of the stair, thin laminations of Douglas fir are clamped and glued into a handrail blank.

laminations can take a lot of force, and pipe clamps are handy for the initial bending. Then I check for gaps between plies and clamp where I find one—any unglued gaps can later split the whole rail open. The 40 or so clamps I have are barely enough for a 10-ft. bend. Once the rail is aligned and clamped to my satisfaction, I let it cure for 24 hours. With this staircase, I repeated the operation for the other length of rail.

I clamp the cured handrail in my bench vise and square up the rail cross section with rasps, planes, and scrapers. This operation is easy enough, but the next operation—shaping the rail—is not. Although I have a custom-made ogee router

Spiral-Stair Layout

For a spiral stair of any given diameter and floor-to-floor rise, there is an optimum unit rise and number of treads per revolution. You find these two numbers by applying the standard rise-to-run formula to the stair at its walkline.

The rise-to-run formula is: two times the rise plus the run should total 24 in. to 25 in. Also, the maximum comfortable incline for a spiral stair is considered to be 45°, at which point the rise equals the run. In our formula, a 45° stairway would result if the rise and run were both 8 in. to 8½ in.

The walkline is the line followed by a person using the stair, and for treads less than 36 in. wide this is generally taken as the centerline of the stair. The length of the walkline provides the basic measure from which the length of run is calculated. This stair has an outside diameter of 72 in., or a radius of 36 in. Its walkline radius is therefore 18 in., and the walkline length in one full revolution is the circumference of a circle with an 18-in. radius. The circumference of a circle is found with the formula $2\pi \times \text{radius}$. For this stair, the walkline circumference is therefore 113 in. The minimum desirable run of a tread is about 8 in., so I divided 113 in. by 8 in. to get the number of treads needed per revolution for the stair. The answer is 14.1, which I rounded to 14 treads per revolution.

This staircase has a total rise of 106 in. The fact that the run was about 8 in. dictated a rise of about 8 in. Because 106÷8 = 13.25 rises, I rounded down to 13 rises, resulting in a unit rise of 8.156 in. There were to be 13 rises, so the stair would spiral less than one revolution. It would have 12 treads, with the 13th step being the landing.

One final layout concern should not be overlooked. I have seen designers specify a 12-tread-per-revolution stair with a 90° arc (quarter-circle) landing at the top. This is generally not desirable because of headroom considerations. Imagine descending such a stair. As you reach the front edge of the ninth tread down, you are faced with the back edge of the landing above you. As you step off the ninth tread, will your head clear the landing? It will—but only if you're short. The accepted figure for headroom on a stair is 80 in. In order for nine steps to drop you 80 in., the unit rise would have to be about 9 in., assuming the landing had very little thickness to further encroach on headroom. Most codes allow a 9-in. rise for a spiral stair, but as I explained above, such a stair would be very steep. The best solution to this problem is to cut back the landing to a 60° arc.

An excellent book on spiral-stair layout is *Designing Staircases*, by Willibald Mannes, (Van Nostrand Reinhold, out of print). In it, Mannes presents diagrams summarizing the optimum layout for stairs of varying diameters and heights.

Shaping the handrail. White makes several passes with a custom ogee bit to shape the handrail. The groove in the underside of the rail was cut with a 1-in. straight bit.

Rail return. At the landing, the handrail engages the wall by way of a curved section cut from a solid piece of stock. Its bolt hold is plugged with a dowel.

Laminating Requires Speed and Preparation

I have always managed to glue up all the plies of a spiral rail at once, but I have to work fast. I lay out all my pipe clamps and C-clamps near the cylinders, set all the laminations side by side in the right order on a flat surface with the center marked on each piece, and check that I have plenty of glue.

One time, incredibly, I ran out of glue partway into the spreading. Luckily, a friend was helping, and he spread what glue we had while I raced to the nearest hardware store, where I stood in line, twitching with adrenalin flashes as I pondered the uses of a partially laminated handrail. But I only lost about five minutes, and the glue-up was saved.

bit (made by Oakland Carbide) to shape the rail with a minimum of passes, the rail has no flat surface to guide the router. I compensate for this by warping the plastic router base with shims to conform to the twist of the rail (see the left photo above). But the operation requires a steady hand. After routing, I use sandpaper and plenty of elbow grease to finish the handrail sections. Last, the upper length of handrail needed a wall-return piece at the landing (see the right photo above) which I attached with a standard rail bolt.

The balusters on this stair are 1-in. square spindles. On any stair or landing, I try to keep the space between the balusters to no more than 4½ in. both for the safety of any children using the stair and for looks. In this case I used three balusters per tread. I machined round tenons at the base of each baluster to fit into holes drilled into the treads, but left the tops long to be cut on site.

This stair has three newel posts: a starting newel and two landing newels. I made them from 4x4s, bandsawing a four-sided taper in the mid-section (see the photo on p. 107). A commercially made ball top caps each newel. One of the landing newels sits atop the center column and has a tenon at its base to fit into the column.

Pulling It All Together

I began the installation with the second-floor landing. Ledgers screwed to adjacent walls provided support for three of its four corners. The fourth corner bore on a dado in the stair column. This intersection was further strengthened with a lag bolt.

Once I had the landing in place, I temporarily installed the column. Making sure that the column was plumb, I traced around it at the floor. Then I removed the column and screwed a wooden disc the diameter of the inside of the column to the floor. I slipped the column over this disc and tethered the top of the column to the landing with a rope. This allowed me to rotate the column as I inserted the treads. A rotating column isn't necessary if there is good access to all sides of the stair.

Installing the treads is the fun part of the job (see the photo on p. 116). I start at the bottom, pushing each one home and then drawing it tight to the column with a ⅜-in. by 7-in. lag bolt. Once all the treads are in place, I permanently lag-bolt the column to the landing and plug the recessed bolt holes with dowels.

Balustrade assembly began with the newel posts. Once they were in place, I was ready to join the two lengths of spiral handrail. To determine their finished length, I laid them in position atop the treads and marked them where they overlapped. Then I square-cut the two abutting ends and joined the pieces with glue and a rail bolt (see the left photo on p. 117). Next, I bevel-cut the tops of several balusters to 32 in. These balusters were inserted through the front hole of several treads and temporarily braced plumb. This would establish the top of the handrail at 34 in. above the nosings of the treads. Setting the spiral rail on top of the balusters, I screwed the downstairs end of the handrail to the starting newel. This intersection is further strengthened with a ½-in. dowel. Upstairs, the handrail engages the wall with a return that is Molly-bolted to the wall. Toenailing the balusters into the rail fixed it in position, and I could then fill in the rest of the balusters. I measured and cut each one individually to ensure a tight, plum fit.

The balusters that extend through the front of each tread and into the tread below were fixed in place by dowels driven horizontally into each tread. They help link the entire assembly into a single unit, reducing the tendency of individual treads to wiggle as they are stepped on. Although it looks like it would be impossible to install these balusters with the handrail in place, there was no problem. They are flexible enough to bend out of the plane of the handrail as they are driven home with a hammer and a wooden block (see the bottom right photo on p. 117).

To stiffen the balustrade at the bottom of the stair, I drove a ⅜-in. steel pin through the rail and into a stud in the wall. Fortuitously, a stud was located adjacent to the rail's closest proximity to the wall.

Sources

Oakland Carbide
1232 51st Ave.
Oakland, CA 94601
(415) 532-7669

Daly's Inc.
3525 Stone Way N.
Seattle, WA 98103
(800) 521-0714

The fun part. Once the column has been slipped over its base and tethered to the landing, White can insert the numbered treads into their mortises, and the stair quickly takes shape. Note the dadoes above the mortises at the top of the column. The dadoes accept the ends of the treads, making a clean joint and reducing wiggle.

I finished up by fairing the joint between the handrail sections to make a smooth transition. Then I applied three coats of Daly's Floor-Fin (a urethane and tung-oil finish) to the entire stair. I like the way this finish looks, and it's easy to apply—it's a brush-on and wipe-off finish. It's also formulated to hold up to the rigors of foot traffic.

Steven M. White was a designer, carpenter, and woodworker who specialized in staircases. He now designs and builds fine furniture from his shop in Bishop, CA.

Rail-to-newel. At the starting newel, the handrail is affixed with a ½-in. dowel and a 2-in. galvanized drywall screw.

Pass-through balusters. The leading baluster on each tread passes through a mortise to engage the tread below it. White used a 1-in. chisel to square the mortises.

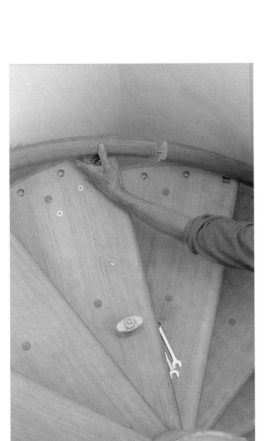

Handrail joint. Handrail sections are joined with a rail bolt. A hole in the underside of the upper rail allows access to tighten a nut onto the bolt's machine-threaded end.

Capping a Curved Stair Wall

■ BY JOHN GRIFFIN

had contracted the finish stair work on a large spec house in Boulder, Colorado, basing my estimate on the blueprints. When I showed up to start work, though, I realized I had to toss that estimate out the window. The job had apparently gotten much simpler.

I wouldn't have to build curved stringer stairs with mitered risers and miter-returned treads. The framing contractor had built both curved staircases leading from the foyer to the second floor. And 34-in.-high 2x4 kneewalls took the place of the massive round newels and 2-in. pipe rails specified on the prints. Then the builder, Vaughn Paul, asked me to finish the curved kneewalls with maple caps. He wanted the caps to bend around the stair's radius without showing laminations on their tops. The caps were to meet the drywall cleanly—no trim. My mind raced. How was I to bend helical twists into 1½-in.-thick, 7-in.-wide boards without visible laminations or trim?

Hiding Lamination Stripes

The author laminated the curving cap from wide, thin stock. The layers are hidden on the side, where they're less visible than they would be on the cap's top.

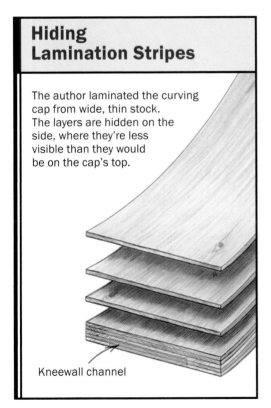

Kneewall channel

The cap had to be laminated; there was no other way to bend it. I reasoned that even maple, as hard and dense as it is, flexes if thin enough. If the stock were, say, 3/16 in. thick and 12 in. wide, I might be able to glue and clamp a horizontal lamination into the correct twist, then saw it to the helical shape (see the drawing below). The laminations would show on the edges, but not on the face.

Gluing Two Layers at a Time

My hardwood supplier resawed some 12-in. boards into 3/16-in. thicknesses for me. But even at 3/16 in. thick, maple is tough. Figuring that less material would be easier to bend, I rough-sawed the curves to within ¼ in. of their finished dimension into the individual laminations (see the drawing on p. 121). Even so, I could clamp and glue the bend into only two laminations at a time. I used Titebond Supreme from Franklin International, spreading it with cheap, disposable paintbrushes. This special-order glue has a long working time, and it's easier on sanding belts than regular Titebond.

I screwed cauls (see the drawing on p. 120) on 4½-in. centers to the plywood top plate with 3½-in. drywall screws, and used additional 1x2 cauls on top of the lamination to spread the clamping pressure evenly (see the photo on p. 121). It took eight days and all my clamps to glue up the two 5-ft.-long twisting boards.

When the final lamination cured, I unclamped the caps and unscrewed the cauls. Placing the caps atop the kneewalls, I traced the wall's outline on their underside. The finished cap was to project 1¼ in. beyond each side of the wall, so I set my

How was I to bend helical twists into 1½-in.-thick, 7-in.-wide boards without visible laminations or trim?

Forming a Fair Curve

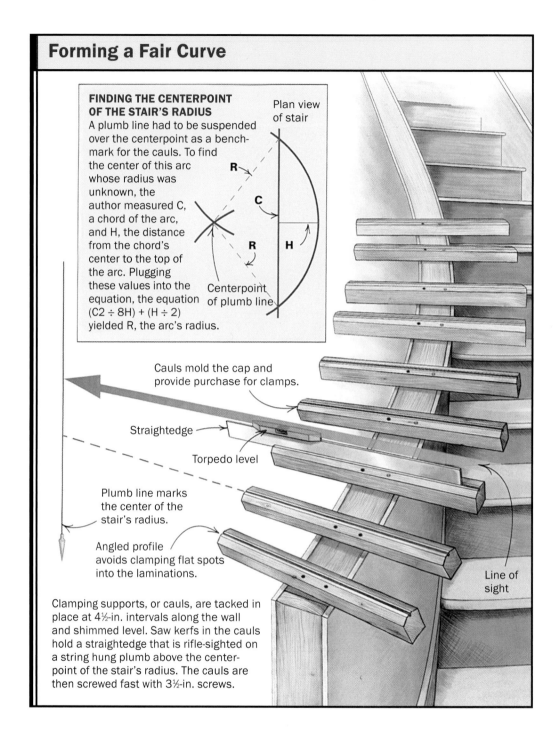

FINDING THE CENTERPOINT OF THE STAIR'S RADIUS
A plumb line had to be suspended over the centerpoint as a benchmark for the cauls. To find the center of this arc whose radius was unknown, the author measured C, a chord of the arc, and H, the distance from the chord's center to the top of the arc. Plugging these values into the equation, the equation $(C2 \div 8H) + (H \div 2)$ yielded R, the arc's radius.

Plan view of stair

R

C

R

H

Centerpoint of plumb line

Cauls mold the cap and provide purchase for clamps.

Straightedge

Torpedo level

Plumb line marks the center of the stair's radius.

Angled profile avoids clamping flat spots into the laminations.

Line of sight

Clamping supports, or cauls, are tacked in place at 4½-in. intervals along the wall and shimmed level. Saw kerfs in the cauls hold a straightedge that is rifle-sighted on a string hung plumb above the centerpoint of the stair's radius. The cauls are then screwed fast with 3½-in. screws.

compass to the overhang and scribed the finished width from the wall.

I bandsawed the curves, staying about ⅟₁₆ in. outside of the scribed lines to leave room for final sanding and truing. I didn't use a jigsaw because I feared the blade would wander.

Routing the Cap to Hide the Drywall Edge

To fit the caps over the top of the kneewall and to hide the drywall edges, I plowed a ½-in. deep, 4½-in. wide channel in their underside. I began by kerfing the caps with a circular saw to remove some of the material. Then, using a ¾-in. straight carbide bit in my router, I finished the channel, carefully

Less Material Bends Easier

To mark out and remove the waste before glue up, the first lamination was clamped in place and the curve of the wall scribed on its bottom with a compass. The waste was cut away, and this piece served as a template to mark the succeeding layers.

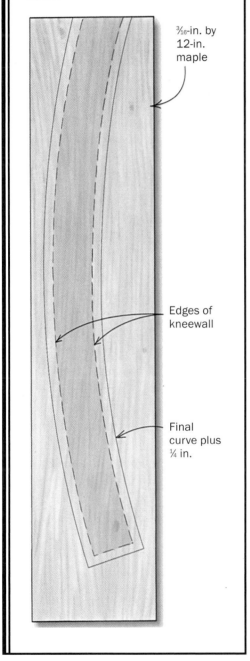

³⁄₁₆-in. by 12-in. maple

Edges of kneewall

Final curve plus ¼ in.

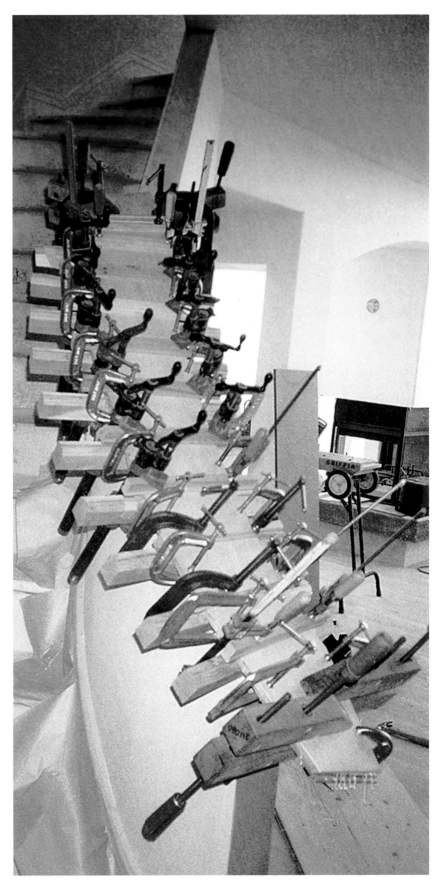

Gluing up. Even after the excess material was cut away, the maple proved to be so tough that only two layers could be glued at a time.

Sources

Franklin International
2020 Bruck St.
Columbus, OH 43207
(800) 669-4583
Titebond Supreme

Cutting a Channel in the Cap's Bottom

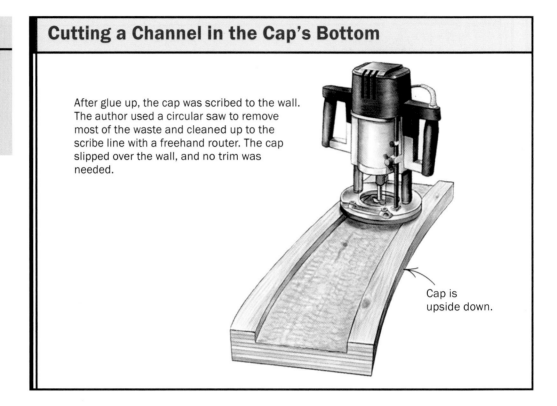

After glue up, the cap was scribed to the wall. The author used a circular saw to remove most of the waste and cleaned up to the scribe line with a freehand router. The cap slipped over the wall, and no trim was needed.

Cap is upside down.

With the cap temporarily screwed in place, the edges were sanded square and to their final shape.

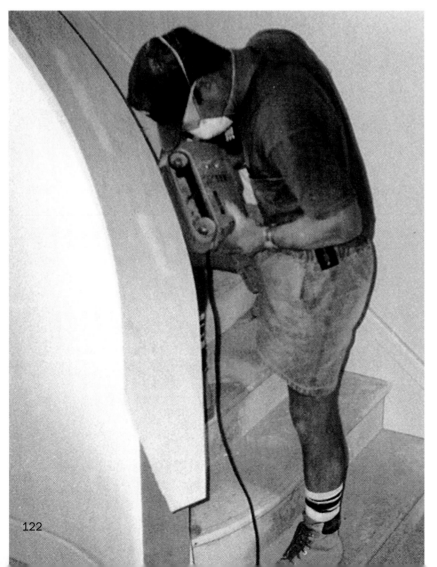

cutting to the kneewall pencil lines (see the drawing above). Freehanding a router on a twisted board isn't easy, but I took my time and was pleased with the results.

After temporarily reinstalling the caps on the wall, I spent a day fairing and squaring their edges with a belt sander. I checked the edges frequently with a combination square as I sanded. Finally, I plowed a matching channel in the bottom of the straight sections on the table saw and rounded over all the edges. I butt-joined the straight sections to the curve, reinforcing the joints with #20 biscuits. Construction adhesive and 2½-in. screws hold the cap to the wall, and ⅜-in. face-grain plugs fill the screw holes.

John Griffin is a finish carpenter who lives in Louisville, CO.

Framing Curved Stairs on Site

■ BY SCOTT PASCHAL

Construction is too specialized today. I once worked for a construction company where we did all the carpentry ourselves, from demolition to trim. I like working in this kind of environment. There is a real motivation to maintain quality. If I am tempted to leave out a difficult piece of blocking while framing, thinking about trying to nail crown molding to air puts me right back on track. Even so, we usually subcontracted the stairs.

Looking over blueprints for the whole-house remodel we were doing, we saw that the main stairs would be difficult. They curved, and their radius changed halfway up. We solicited bids from several stair-builders, expecting to be able to choose based on price and delivery date.

The curves of this finished stair hide its straight skeleton. Built without the rushed panic of gluing a laminated stringer and using methods a journeyman carpenter can master, these stairs look like the product of a master stairbuilder.

Sources

Calculated Industries, Inc.
4840 Hytech Dr.
Carson City, NV 89706
(775) 885-4900
www.calculated.com
Scale Master®

Someone Has to Build Them

Only one stairbuilder submitted a bid, and it was high. This setback, combined with our desire to do most of the work in-house, led us to build the stairs ourselves on site.

Four constraints made this staircase challenging. The stairs had to fit in a confined area. Then, the plans called for the stairs' radius to change: The lower half would have a 6-ft. inside radius, and the upper a much tighter 1-ft. 6-in. inside radius. Next, a closet was planned under the upper section, and of course, everything had to meet the current building code.

Our first job was enlarging the stairwell opening in the second floor to accommodate the larger stair. Then we built the platform where the stairs would land on the first floor; it stepped down to the living room, and its edge was a modified French curve. The platform's right side curved into what would become the inside wall of the stairs, creating an area for the handrail volute. We drew the French curve by eye on a piece of ¾-in. plywood, cut it with a jigsaw and used this pattern for the 2x top and bottom plates. We framed the edge of the platform like a kneewall, using 2x4 cripple studs.

The main body of this platform was framed conventionally—2x8 joists with ¾-in. tongue-and-groove plywood glued and nailed to them. The living room, landing, and stair treads all would have ¾-in. oak flooring installed later. We used standard strip flooring on the stairs to avoid wide glued-up treads.

Using Chalklines and Story Poles to Lay Out the Stair

Two existing straight walls at 90° to each other defined the outside of the stairs (see the drawing at left). The double curve that defined the inside of the stairs was more difficult. The blueprints showed the locations of two centerpoints for radii to establish the inner curves and specified where on the staircase the radius changed. Once we found the centerpoints, we used compasses made from 1x4s to draw two connecting arcs on the floor. We snapped lines on the floor representing the stairwell opening, which, with the two back walls and two intersecting arcs, provided us the outline of the stair in its opening.

We then calculated the riser height and tread widths. The total rise of 105⅞ in. divided by 14 risers gave us a 7%₆-in. rise per step. Next, we measured the length of the two arcs with a digital estimating tool, essentially

Full-Scale Layout Helped to Visualize This Complex Stair

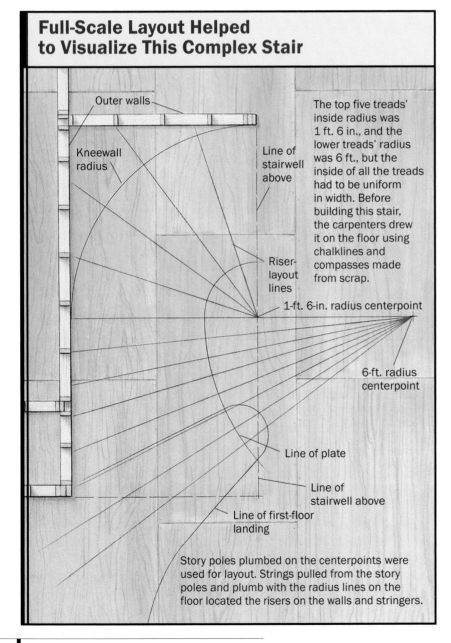

Outer walls

Kneewall radius

Line of stairwell above

The top five treads' inside radius was 1 ft. 6 in., and the lower treads' radius was 6 ft., but the inside of all the treads had to be uniform in width. Before building this stair, the carpenters drew it on the floor using chalklines and compasses made from scrap.

Riser-layout lines

1-ft. 6-in. radius centerpoint

6-ft. radius centerpoint

Line of plate

Line of stairwell above

Line of first-floor landing

Story poles plumbed on the centerpoints were used for layout. Strings pulled from the story poles and plumb with the radius lines on the floor located the risers on the walls and stringers.

Starting with a French curve. The landing platform for these stairs ends in a graceful curve that the author laid out by eye and built like a short stud wall.

a wheel on a handle that is rolled along, giving a digital readout of the distance and usually used for plan takeoffs (Scale Master, Calculated Industries, Inc.). The measurement was 85⁵⁄₁₆ in., divided by the number of treads—13—which calculated to 6⁹⁄₁₆ in. per tread. The building code states that a pie-shaped tread can't be any less than 6 in. at its narrowest, so this was perfect. Using the digital estimating tool again, we put a mark every 6⁹⁄₁₆ in. on our curves.

Next, we snapped lines from the two centerpoints through these marks on the curves to the outside walls. These chalklines represented the fronts of the risers and radiated from the two centerpoints like the spokes of a wheel. We plumbed and braced a 2x4 story pole at each of the two centerpoints. The story poles were marked every 7⁹⁄₁₆ in. to represent the rise of each step.

Straight stringers support this curved stair. A header carries the three stringers used on the lower section of this stair. The kneewall in the middle provides additional support.

Studs take the place of a laminated stringer. These curved stairs have no laminated stringer. Studs rise from a curved plate to support the treads and risers.

Framing the Lower Stairs

The outside wall at the 6-ft. radius section was straight—only the inside wall curved here. Three straight stringers were used to carry the outside and the center of the stairs. The treads and risers at the inner curved area were supported by a stud wall.

Because the treads widen from inside to out, the notch in the outside stringer would be deep. We needed beefy stock, so we used 1¾-in. by 11⅞-in. laminated beams. The stairs get wider at the bottom, so the stringers aren't parallel to each other. This variance, combined with the widening tread, made it impossible to step off the stringers with a framing square. We needed a way to mark each riser and its angle of cut on the stringers.

We determined where the upper and lower sections would meet by plumbing up from the chalklines on the floor and leveling over from the story pole. We framed a kneewall and a header there to carry the lower stringers (see the top photo). We figured the overall length of the stringers by measuring from our layout lines on the floor to the header. We then made the top and bottom cuts on the stringers and set them in place.

To lay out the treads and risers on the stringers, we plumbed up from the chalklines and leveled over from the story pole again. By pulling a string over the stringers from the story pole to the points where the bottoms of the treads and the backs of the risers meet, we could mark the cut angle for the risers and notch the stringers. Next we built the bottom plate for the inside wall by stacking three pieces of ¾-in. plywood cut to the radius marked on the floor. This plate was thicker than the usual 1½ in. to give us better nailing for the curved baseboard that would come later. The studs for the curved wall were placed to support the ends of each tread and riser (see the bottom photo on the facing page). To complete the framing of the lower part of the stairs, ¾-in. plywood sub-treads and risers were glued and then stapled in place.

Stairs without Stringers

We had to build the upper section with no stringers to provide headroom in the closet below. Stringers would have taken too much space. The radius was too tight for straight stringers, anyway.

We started by framing the inner wall, us-ing the story pole and chalklines for refer-ence just as we did on the lower stair. The inner-wall studs carry single 2x10s on edge under the back of each tread, and we nailed these 2x10s to the ledgers on the outside wall. Blocking then was screwed between these 2x10s and the risers, and ¾-in. ply-wood subtreads were glued and stapled to all. As each step was completed, the next riser was placed over the 2x10 at the back of the lower tread (see the top photo), and the process was repeated.

After all the treads, blocking, and supports were in place, the last bit of framing was building a section of curved wall in the corner of the upper stair (see the bottom photo). We drew an arc with the upper story pole as its center on the treads, maintaining the stair width. We followed this arc with a short wall that we capped at two levels for plant shelves.

Finishing the Stairs

The finish skirtboards were bent from kerfed medium-density fiberboard and scribed to fit the subtreads and subrisers. We made the

Winding stairs without a stringer. Two-by-tens, resting on the inner wall and fastened to ledgers on the outer wall with framing hardware, sup-port the treads and risers.

A curved kneewall forms plant shelves. Stepping up with the stairs, this kneewall supports two platforms that will later be used to display plants.

tread nosings from 5/4 stock, following the inside radii of the treads and the French curve of the landing. We rabbeted the backs of the nosings to a ¼-in. thickness that matched the oak flooring we used for the treads themselves.

We bent the curved risers from ¼-in. ply-wood. This worked well on most of the curves, but in some places the radius was tight enough that we had to kerf the back of the plywood to keep it from breaking. Work-ing from the bottom up, we placed the risers, nosings, and finish flooring. Finally, we nailed the scotias—the molding under the nosing—and called in the railing contractor. We just didn't have enough clamps to lami-nate a curved railing.

Scott Paschal has been working in the construction industry for 26 years. He is currently construction manager and superintendent for Gregg Custom Builders in Denver, CO.

We had to build the upper section with no stringers to provide headroom in the closet below.

Cantilevered Stairway

■ BY ROB HARLAN

No visible means of support. Projecting from a curved wall, this custom ash stair is supported by cantilevered steel brackets housed in the tread supports. The treads are glued and screwed to the supports, and the balustrade of bent laminations not only enhances the organic look but also helps stiffen the stair.

Curves make my heart sing. When I built my own house, one of the things I did was to frame a 16-ft.-diameter, two-story cylindrical room. The curving wall was a great place to locate the stairway. I had a picture of a curved adobe building with slabs of wood for stair treads cantilevered out through the wall. I wanted to build a similar stair, but the problem was how to capture the adobe-house stair's light, suspended feeling, yet have it structurally sound and in compliance with the building code.

Steel Solves the Problem

I tried a whole bunch of wood-based designs, but the only one that worked involved extending the cantilevers through the other side of the wall, and that created space problems. Then, a friend suggested using steel to support the stair treads. Being primarily a woodworker, I had to be talked into it, but steel made for strong cantilevers that I could contain within the 2x6 wall.

I had a machinist make stair-support brackets from ¼-in. by 4-in. plate steel. Most of the brackets are two plates lapped and welded to form a T-shape. The top of the T is fastened to the studs with four ½-in. machine bolts; the base of the T protrudes through the curved wall and supports the treads (see the photo above). An engineer OK'd the bracket design, and the building department approved the stair.

The brackets are not all T-shaped. The bottom two are L-shaped, and the top ones are attached to the second-story floor joists, so they're straight.

Brackets fit in the wall. The doubled 2x6 studs were laid out on 9³⁄₁₆-in. centers—the run of the stairs at the wall—so that a welded-steel bracket could be bolted to each stud.

One Stud Per Tread

The cylindrical room was framed with 2x6s on 16-in. centers. In the area where the stairs project from the curved wall, I used doubled 2x6s to make 3-in. by 5½-in. studs on 9³⁄₁₆-in. centers at the outside edge. Each of these studs bears a stair bracket.

The stud spacing is based on some fairly simple math. The stairs are laid out with a 6¹³⁄₁₆-in. rise and an 11-in. run. Because the treads are wedge shaped, the run is longer out at the railing than at the wall. The 11-in. run is at the center of the tread, where one is most likely to walk. All I had to do was figure out the run at the wall.

I knew the radius of the circle to the outer edge of the stud wall (96 in.). I also knew the radius of the circle at the center of the treads (115¼ in.). I knew the run of the stairs at the center of the treads (11 in.). I determined stud spacing with a ratio: $115.25 \div 11 = 96 \div x$. The radius and the run at the center of the treads are directly proportional to the radius and the run at the wall. Putting in the numbers yielded 9³⁄₁₆-in. o. c. for the stud spacing.

Drywall went on first. Slits were cut in the plywood-and-drywall sheathing materials so that the brackets could be reinstalled from inside the cylindrical room.

The double studs were marked at the correct heights, using a builder's level and a story pole, and then drilled out for the bolts that secure the steel brackets to the studs. The lapped portions of the brackets were let into the studs so that the brackets could be bolted tight to the studs.

After walking up and down the supports a few times to verify their soundness and checking the layout for consistency of spacing, rise and levelness, I unbolted the brackets, rubbed them with stove black to prevent rust, and stored them.

As construction progressed, I wrapped the outside of the curved wall with ⅜-in. CDX plywood and later with ½-in. drywall (see the photo above). Slits were cut through these wall coverings, and eventually the steel supports were reinstalled from the back and bolted into position permanently before the drywall on the other side of the wall was installed.

Supporting the Treads

I chose white ash for the entire stairway—the tread supports, the treads, and the balustrade—because of its light color, durability, and bendability.

Each tread support consists of three pieces of 5⁄4 by 6-in. ash sandwiched over the steel bracket. The outer section of the tread support was mortised with a router to create a pocket to house the steel (see the photo on the facing page). The tread support was glued with Titebond ES747 and screwed to the steel, which had been drilled with eight ⅛-in. countersunk holes.

The remaining two sections of the tread supports were glued with Weldwood® urea resin and screwed to the outer piece, covering the steel. Great care was taken to assemble the tread supports around the steel so that the joints were flush and to clean up all glue drippage with water immediately to minimize sanding after assembly.

I tapered the tread supports with a bandsaw, then planed, routed, sanded, and installed them. Tapering gives the suspended staircase the light look I wanted.

Although the steel brackets cantilever through the wall, the wooden tread supports were installed on top of the finished wall, which provided for easier plastering and painting. It also kept any movement of the stairs from cracking the plaster. To give the stairway its "coming out of the wall" look, I caulked where the tread supports met the wall with flexible caulk and then carefully painted it.

Tread supports sandwich the brackets.
The three-piece ash tread support was mortised and fastened to the steel with Titebond ES747 construction adhesive and screws. Weldwood urea resin glue and screws bonded the tread support, which provides bearing for the treads.

Making Treads

The treads are 8/4 by 12-in. pie-shaped pieces blind-splined together from 6-in. wide stock. The splines are ⅛-in. by 1½-in. pieces of white ash placed in ⅛-in. slots in the treads. Both the splines and the slots were made with a table saw.

The treads were glued and screwed to the tread supports. I left a uniform ¼-in. gap between the finished wall and the end of the tread to heighten the floating feeling.

Once again, I countersunk the screws and plugged the holes. The landing was made similarly by gluing and splining many pie-shaped pieces together.

Laminated Balustrade

The balustrade I designed for this stairway preserves the light, suspended feeling of the cantilevers and weaves them together, which stiffens them. Each baluster consists of a pair of bent laminations. I made two separate bending forms, one for each baluster shape, then glued up twelve ³⁄₃₂-in.-wide strips of ash and clamped them in the forms.

Once the glue had cured, the bent laminations were trued up using a table saw to clean and cut the edges square, then finished with a belt sander and rounded over with a router and lots of hand sanding. Next, the balusters were glued, screwed, and plugged together at their bases to form pairs.

The handrail was laminated from eight ⁵⁄₁₆-in. by 1¼-in. by 16-ft.-long strips of ash. The problem was figuring out the radius of the handrail and how to bend it. The process turned out to be easy. I didn't have to use math; I laminated the rail in place using the outside ends of the treads as a form to hold the railing in the correct bend. The strips were clamped together with C-clamps every 3 in. It's moments such as these when you use all of your clamps and any that you can borrow.

Once the railing lamination was sanded and routed to its final shape, I set it temporarily in place. The baluster assemblies were carefully marked and cut to fit below it. I attached the balusters to the railing with ¼-in. by 2-in. dowels. The base of each baluster was mortised into the tread and glued and screwed to it.

When the balustrade was complete, the entire structure stiffened up considerably, and my dream of an organic, strong, light, curved stairway was achieved.

Rob Harlan is a licensed general and solar contractor in Mendocino, CA.

A Stair in the Air

■ BY GLEN STEWART

I have the best client in the world. He likes only the simplest designs for the projects he commissions. And let no degree of complexity stand in the way of those projects.

One particularly interesting project was the stairway in his new home on Nantucket. John, a.k.a. "best client," claimed that a standard set of stairs supported with framework underneath not only would destroy the character of the hallway entry but that a closed-in stairwell would also make the hallway narrow and claustrophobic. So John suggested eliminating risers between the stairs to let more light pass through.

I've always been intrigued with the idea of stringerless stairs and ways of supporting tread load by other means. So I suggested going one step further and getting rid of the stringers as well. The stair would then be reduced to its three basic elements: treads, handrails, and balusters. Could it be any simpler?

Engineering Support

Several designs of stringerless stairs use steel cantilevered from a wall. But most of these designs have an angle brace under the tread to transfer the load back to the wall. We agreed that this brace interfered with simplicity, the visible steel brackets adding another structural element. Plus, we wanted to keep the treads to a minimal thickness and keep all the structural elements hidden. What to do?

Lucky for me, John, in his role as "best client," has wonderful taste in wine, and we decided to drink some, and have dinner, too. Have I mentioned that any candidate vying for position as best client in the world should have a gracious spouse who is a talented cook? At dinner, we let the wine and food help us to explore our options.

Before I go any further, I should explain that John is an engineer, the kind who drinks coffee before he goes to sleep. The next morning, John called with a potential solution. He described a system of steel brackets made of flat bar stock that could be attached to the wall framing and be buried

in the treads and balusters. The top of each bracket would be bolted to the nose of the tread above while the bottom of the bracket was bolted to the heel of the tread below. The idea sounded reasonable to me.

That afternoon, a fax arrived at my office with the load-deflection calculations, a finite-element stress analysis with bending modes and, of course, graphic interpretations in a gray scale. Unfortunately, I don't have a color fax. Does anyone?

As a well-trained carpenter and surfer used to hiding my ignorance with chameleonlike grace and mimicked terminology, I called John back, thanked him for the fax, mumbled something unintelligible about error analysis, asked if he thought he carried his transforms through enough iterations and, by the way, "How thick was that steel?"

"A quarter-inch."

"And how wide?"

"Inch and a quarter."

"Oh, good, that's what I came up with, too."

Testing Begins

A week later, the prototypes of the steel brackets arrived from the fabricator, and we built a test section in my shop. Armed with a stringline, a story pole, a tape measure, and a skeptical 200-lb. test subject, we measured deflection. We were aiming for zero.

"Three-sixteenths? Yikes! How could that happen?"

Careful observation showed that the steel itself performed as expected, but there were two unexpected problems (see the drawing on pp. 136-137). First, the wall studs were deflecting in an S pattern, and second, the cantilevered ends of the steel brackets were twisting out of plane.

We eliminated stud deflection by replacing the standard 2x6 studs with 1¾-in. by 5½-in. laminated-veneer lumber (LVL). Also, the plate that fastened the steel box bracket to the stud was lengthened to 48 in. with ½-in.-dia. through bolts in zero-clearance

holes. We also decided to glue and screw a ¾-in. plywood skin to the backside of the studs so that the load was distributed to more than one stud.

The other contribution to deflection was more subtle, a result of the steel twisting out of plane when load was applied. The addition of balusters and handrail would keep the cantilevered end of the steel bracket from twisting, eliminating this movement. The handrail-baluster system was no longer

Open-Tread Stairs and Building Codes

At the time we designed and started these stairs, Nantucket was using the 1988 UBC codebook, which required that the maximum opening in the stairs could not allow a 6-in. sphere to pass through. The new code decreased the size of the sphere to 4 in. and was adopted by Nantucket during construction of this stair.

The issue of baluster spacing never came up during any of the inspections. But we did have a contingency plan to add ¾-in.-dia. dowels between the balusters if the problem arose; fortunately, it never did because the dowels would have complicated the aesthetics of the stair.

The building code treats open risers the same as the openings between balusters, so the 51¹⁄₁₆ in. between treads satisfied code at the time. We didn't have a strategy for changing the openings between treads, but with my client, the engineer, I'm sure we would have come up with an elegant solution.

Installing the Brackets Was Easy

We were now ready for installation of the framing and steel at John's house. The framing of the wall required precise layout. The face of each stud had to be located exactly 1½ in. back from the finished nose of each tread, 9⅝ in. o. c.

Likewise, the steel frames had to be bolted carefully to each LVL stud to produce the 7³⁄₁₆-in. rise (see the photo at left). After a painstaking installation of the studs and steel brackets, we bolted temporary treads in place and went away while the real work was being done. God bless all electricians, plumbers, plasterers, floor guys, and painters.

Steel Brackets Disappear behind Wood

The flooring for the house was southern yellow pine, a common choice for the area, so we chose the same for the treads. Cherry handrails and ash balusters were chosen to match John's furniture.

I had wanted to use solid 1½-in.-thick stock for the treads, but working on an island has its own special problems: This stock just wasn't available. So I convinced myself that two layers of ¾-in. stock were better than solid stock because the opposing grain patterns would counter each other's stresses and make the treads more stable. An inch and a half was cut from the nose and heel of each tread and carefully labeled to be put back on the same tread later. I clamped the middle part of each tread between its nose and heel brackets and marked them for the bolt holes. The treads were then taken out and drilled through from both sides with a self-centering drill guide.

Stairway skeleton. The bones of this stairway are welded-steel brackets bolted to laminated-veneer lumber studs.

just a code requirement and concession to safety: It became a structural necessity.

With these modifications, we now had a working model and were able to say, "See, it works," to all those skeptics, my dog being in that category, while the cat remained consistently aloof. The okay went out to the fabricator for a complete set of the steel-bracket sections. All the brackets were identical except for slight variations in the brackets near the top and bottom of the stairs.

The handrail-baluster system was no longer just a code requirement and concession to safety: It became a structural necessity.

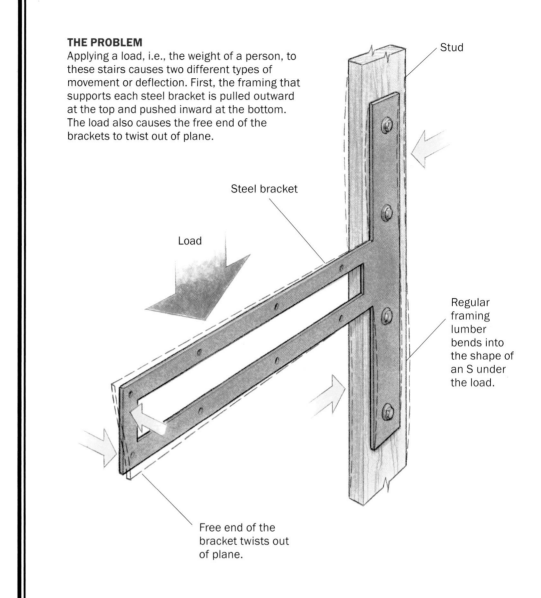

THE PROBLEM
Applying a load, i.e., the weight of a person, to these stairs causes two different types of movement or deflection. First, the framing that supports each steel bracket is pulled outward at the top and pushed inward at the bottom. The load also causes the free end of the brackets to twist out of plane.

Stud

Steel bracket

Load

Regular framing lumber bends into the shape of an S under the load.

Free end of the bracket twists out of plane.

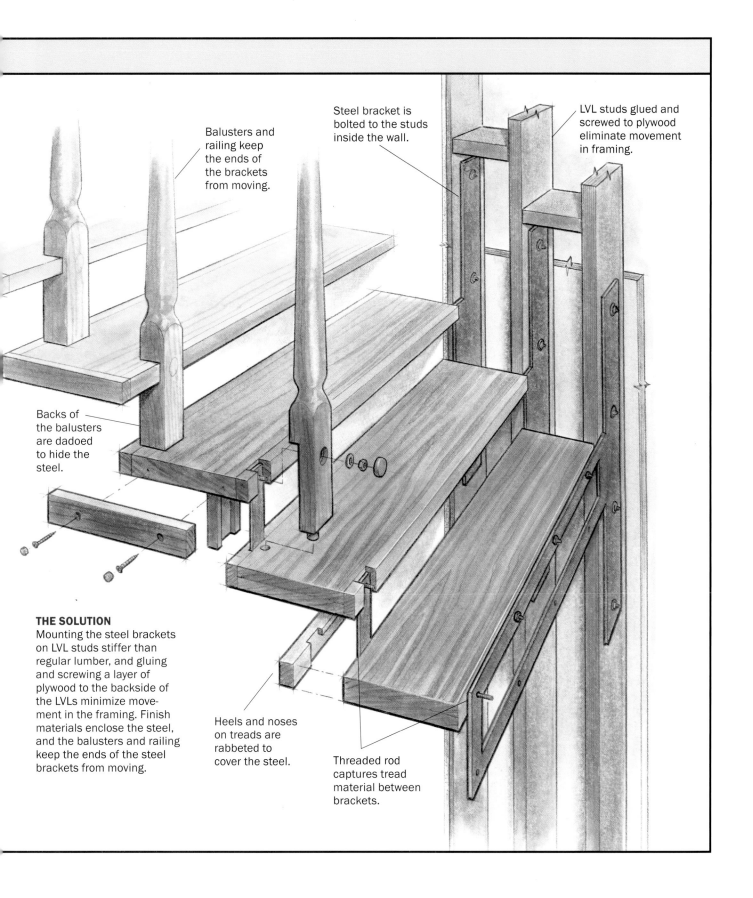

Balusters and railing keep the ends of the brackets from moving.

Steel bracket is bolted to the studs inside the wall.

LVL studs glued and screwed to plywood eliminate movement in framing.

Backs of the balusters are dadoed to hide the steel.

THE SOLUTION
Mounting the steel brackets on LVL studs stiffer than regular lumber, and gluing and screwing a layer of plywood to the backside of the LVLs minimize movement in the framing. Finish materials enclose the steel, and the balusters and railing keep the ends of the steel brackets from moving.

Heels and noses on treads are rabbeted to cover the steel.

Threaded rod captures tread material between brackets.

Stealth balusters. Back sections of the balusters are removed, dadoed to conceal the metal bracket and then reattached. Special care was taken to match the cutoff with the correct baluster.

Fleshing out the stairs. The noses and heels of the permanent treads are removed, rabbeted to wrap over the steel frame and then glued back on. Balusters are bolted in front of the vertical parts of the metal brackets.

To my surprise and relief, most of the holes actually lined up. Quarter-inch threaded rod with a nut and washer on each end captured the treads between opposing steel-bracket sections. I rabbeted the nose and heel pieces to house the steel and counterbored holes for the nuts and washers. The pieces were then glued back on (see the left photo above).

We turned the balusters from 2x2 ash blanks. We left the baluster bottoms square for 9 in. and then cut a ¾-in. by 51⅟₁₆-in. section (distance between the treads) from this square part (see the photo above). These pieces that we cut off the balusters were dadoed to cover the steel and then glued back on in one of the final steps.

Again, we paid careful attention to getting each of these pieces back on the baluster that it was cut from, which left the joint pretty much invisible. The outside tread bolt also passes through the baluster. We counterbored a hole for the nut and washer, which was then hidden by a plug, or bung as my new friends on the East Coast have insisted on calling it.

The finished stair seems simple, but as rewarding as it was to meet this challenge, I don't think I'll build another one. Some things are better left as one of a kind.

Glen Stewart is a carpenter and furnituremaker in Encinitas, CA.

Disappearing Attic Stairways

■ BY WILLIAM T. COX

When I was young and my mother wanted something out of the attic, she would push me up a stepladder and through a little access hole in the ceiling; it was a scary adventure for an 8-year-old, climbing up into a dark, cavelike hole where I thought unknown creatures waited to devour me. What we needed was a disappearing stairway.

Disappearing stairways are available in several styles. All of these stairways have a ceiling-mounted trap door on which the stairway either folds or slides. Nearly all are made of southern yellow pine, although there are a few aluminum disappearing stairways. There are a few commercial models made of aluminum or steel, but this article will concentrate on residential models. Disappearing stairways are not considered to be ladders or staircases, and they do not conform to the codes or the standards of either. Disappearing stairways have their own standards to which they must conform.

Similar to ladders, disappearing stairways have plenty of labels and warnings to read. On all disappearing stairways there are warnings about weight limits because, inevitably, homeowners fall down stairs while trying to carry too much weight into the attic. Also, labels tell the user to tighten the nuts and bolts of the stairway.

Sliding stairway. Disappearing stairways are concealed by a spring-loaded ceiling door. Here, the author walks up a sliding stairway made by Bessler with an angle of incline close to that of a permanent stairway.

In one stairway manufacturer's literature, the word "safer" was used to describe the fluorescent orange paint used on the stairway's treads. But "safer" was replaced by "high visibility" because one homeowner wore off the paint, slipped, and fell. She sued both the manufacturer and the builder because, she claimed, the treads became unsafe to use.

Stairway companies are constantly testing, upgrading, and improving their products to give the consumer the best, safest, and longest-lasting disappearing stairway possible. And with good reason—over a million units were produced in the United States last year.

Folding Stairways

The most popular style of disappearing stairways, folding stairways consist of three ladderlike sections that are hinged together, accordion style. The three sections are attached to a hinged, ceiling-mounted door similar to a trap door. The door and the attached ladderlike sections are held closed to the ceiling by springs on both sides. When you want to access a folding stairway, you pull a cord that is attached to the door and lower the door from the ceiling. The door swings down on a piano hinge. You then grab the two bottom sections of the stairway and pull them toward you, unfolding them (see the photo below). When the two bottom sections are completely unfolded, all three sections butt together at their ends, giving strength and stability to the stairway.

Folding attic stairs are measured by the rough opening they occupy and by the floor-to-ceiling height they will service. The smallest folding stairways are 22 in. wide, and they are made to fit between joists 2 ft. o. c. These narrow stairways are available in models that will service a ceiling height as short as 7 ft., and there are others that can go as high as 12 ft. Keep in mind that a stairway's rough-opening width is appreciably more than the actual width of the ladderlike sections. Because of the attendant jambs, springs, and mounting hardware necessary to operate the stairway, the actual width of the ladderlike section is a lot less than the rough opening. A stairway with a rough opening of 22 in. is going to have a tread about 13 in. wide.

Folding stairways are rated according to weight capacities; the lightest-rated ones will handle 225 lb., and most of the others have a recommended weight capacity of 300 lb. It is interesting to note that American Stairways, Inc., says in its product literature that you are not supposed to carry anything up or down its stairways. Only an unladen person is supposed to climb up or down. This all sounds somewhat ridiculous to me. The reason why people install disappearing stairways is that they can carry stuff up or down from the attic—Christmas ornaments, baby clothes. However, I tell customers not to carry stuff up the folding stairway. You should have someone hand it up to you.

Folding stairway. Ladderlike sections are hinged like an accordion to the ceiling-mounted door. On this model, made by American Stairways, the treads are painted with bright-colored, rubberized paint.

You cannot climb a folding stairway with something in your hands. It's way too steep. I suppose the disclaimer keeps American Stairways out of court if somebody falls down one of the stairways. Also, all folding stairways are for residential use only; a restaurant owner once asked me to install a folding stairway so that he could access a storage area above the kitchen, and I had to refuse.

The smallest folding stairway costs around $75, and the largest, the A-series aluminum folding stairway made by Werner costs around $211. It fits a rough opening of 2 ft. 1½ in. by 4 ft. 6 in. and accommodates a ceiling height of up to 12 ft.

Installing Folding Stairways

Aside from the finish trim, folding stairways come out of the box as a complete, assembled unit. (Other types of stairways require some assembly.) Because most of the installations I do are retrofits into existing buildings, the first thing I must do is cut a hole in the drywall. If possible, I try to mount the stairway alongside an existing joist; this saves some framing work if the stairway is bigger than the space between two joists. Cutting the drywall is not a close-tolerance operation because (within reason) the finish trim will cover any ragged edges. If I have to head off a ceiling joist, I use standard carpentry practices.

Here's a time-saver I came upon after installing quite a few stairways. I've found that it's much easier to cut and fit (but don't nail) the finish trim while the stairway is sitting on the floor in front of me rather than on the ceiling. Leave ⅛ in. between the edge of the door and the jamb. Make sure you mark the location of all four pieces. Once the stairway is installed, you just nail the pieces in place.

Before installing the stairway, I screw two temporary ledgers to the ceiling that project ¾ in. into the rough opening. The ledgers provide a shelf for the stairway's wood frame once I've lifted the unit into the rough opening (see the top photo below). When attaching the ledgers, I make sure they are parallel and that they only stick into the opening ¾ in. Any farther than that, and they might not allow the door to swing open on its piano hinge. Using screws instead of nails to attach the ledger makes it possible to adjust them in case I somehow miscalculate; it also makes them easier to remove when the time comes.

TIP

It's much easier to cut and fit (but don't nail) the finish trim while the stairway is on the floor rather than on the ceiling. Leave ⅛ in. between the edge of the door and the jamb. Make sure you mark the location of all four pieces. Once the stairway is installed, just nail the pieces in place.

Support during installation. Ledgers screwed to the ceiling provide temporary support for the stairway while the author shims and screws the frame to the rough opening.

An extra screw for insurance. A third mounting screw in a folding stairway's piano hinge strengthens the installation. The author drills through the hinge and the jamb and into the rough framing. The large spring at the top of the photo is one of a pair that holds the stairway and its trap door closed to the ceiling.

Measuring for trimming. With the bottom section folded under the middle section, the author puts his weight against the stairway to ensure it is fully extended. He measures along both the top and bottom edges of the stairway, transcribes his measurements on the bottom section, connects the dots and makes his cut. The trap door's pull cord can be seen hanging in the top of the photo.

Although some manufacturers warn against it, I usually remove the bottom two ladderlike sections of the stairway before carrying it up the stepladder. Most often I work alone, and some of the stairways are pretty heavy to lift by myself. A 30-in. by 54-in. stairway made by American Stairways, Inc., weighs 92 lb.

With the ledgers in place, I lift the stairway into the rough opening and set it on the ledgers. Next I carefully open the door fully and center the jamb in the rough opening. Now it's just a matter of shimming the sides of the frame and fastening them to the framing. (Once the unit is installed, I reattach the sections and tighten the nuts and bolts on the hinges with a screwdriver and a socket wrench.)

Most instructions call for nailing the frame in place, but I like to use screws because they are more adjustable than nails, and they are also easier to remove if needed. I start at the hinge end of the stairway jamb. Most folding stairways have a hole drilled at both ends of the piano hinge to screw the hinge into the framing. I always drill another hole through the hinge and sink a third screw (see the photo above). I use #10, 3-in. pan-head screws. Adding a third screw can't hurt, and it only takes an extra minute or two.

Instructions call for screwing or nailing into the framing on both sides of the stairway through two of the holes drilled in the arm plate, which is the metal plate to which the door arms are attached. I shim behind the arm plates because it is critical that the arms stay parallel to the ladder and that the pivot plates remain stationary. If they don't, the rivets that hold the arms will wear out from twisting and torquing as the stairway is used.

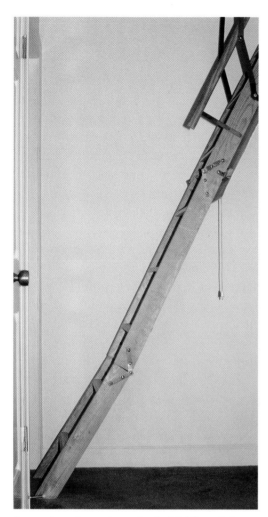

Accurate cuts are important. A folding stairway that is cut too long puts undue stress on the hinges because the ladderlike sections don't butt at their ends.

not difficult to figure out the cut length, but it is critical to the longevity of the stairway that the length be exact. A stairway that is cut too long will not extend to a straight line, and the ends of the ladderlike sections will not butt together (see the photo at left), putting undue stress on the hinges. And a stairway that is cut too short will stress the arm plates, the counterbalancing springs, and the section hinges.

To cut the bottom ladder section to length, I make sure the arms are fully extended and fold the bottom section underneath the middle section. I rest my leg against the stairway to ensure that it is fully extended, and I take my tape measure and hold it along the top, or front, edge of the middle section (see the left photo on the facing page). By extending the end of the tape to the floor (while holding the upper part of the tape against the middle section), I get an exact measurement from the floor to the joint between the two lower sections. I repeat the procedure on the back edge of the stairway to get the length of the back of the cut. Then I remove the lower section, transcribe the measurements and draw a line between the two points on each leg.

After making my cuts and reattaching the bottom section of the stairway, all that's left to do is unscrew the temporary ledgers from the ceiling and run the precut trim around the frame. I've installed quite a few folding stairways, and I can usually manage to do the whole job in about two hours.

Sliding Stairways

Several companies make folding stairways, but Bessler Stairway Company also makes a sliding disappearing stairway. Unlike a folding stairway, where the sections are hinged and fold atop one another, the sliding stairway is one long section that slides on guide bars aided by spring-loaded cables mounted in enclosed drums. When the stairway is closed, the single-section stairway extends beyond the rough opening into the floor

Sliding stairways, unlike folding stairways, are designed so that the user can walk up into the attic while carrying a load.

After I've screwed through the piano hinge and the arm plates, I shut the door and make sure there is an even reveal between the door and the jamb all the way around the door. When this is done I shim and screw off the rest of the wood frame, using #8, 3-in. wood screws.

Cutting Stairs to Length

Because ceiling heights vary, folding attic stairways come in different lengths, and with the exception of aluminum models, you must cut the bottom ladderlike section to length when installing the stairway. It is space above. This is an important consideration because some small attic spaces do not have enough room for the stairway's sliding section.

To access a sliding stairway, you simply pull the door down from the ceiling, similar to the way you'd pull down a folding stairway. Then you grab the single ladderlike section and slide the section toward you, lowering it to the floor. To close the stairway, you slide the single section back up into the opening. A unique cam-operated mechanism locks the ladderlike section in place while you push the door back to the ceiling. A series of spring-loaded, counterbalancing cables makes the door and the ladderlike section feel almost weightless.

The real benefit of sliding stairways is their angle of incline. Folding stairs typically have about a 64° angle of incline. That's pretty steep—more like a ladder than a staircase. Bessler's best sliding stairways have a 53° angle of incline. Sliding stairways, unlike folding stairways, are designed so that the user can walk up into the attic while carrying a load (see the photo on p. 139).

Sliding stairways are made of knot-free southern yellow pine, and there are four different models from which to choose. The smallest—the model 26—has a rough opening of 2 ft. by 4 ft. and has a suggested load capacity of 400 lb. This model has a stairway width of 17 1/16 in. The model 100 requires a rough opening of 2 ft. 6 in. by 5 ft. 6 in. and has a suggested load capacity of 800 lb. The width of the stairway is 18 7/8 in. Sliding stairways are measured from floor to floor, rather than from floor to ceiling like folding stairways, and the largest model 100 will service a floor-to-floor height of 12 ft. 10 in. Sliding stairways also have a full-length handrail.

The smallest sliding stairway, the model 26 with a maximum ceiling height of 7 ft. 10 in., costs around $225. The largest model, the model 100 with a maximum ceiling height of 12 ft. 10 in., costs around $700.

Installing Sliding Stairways

Sliding stairways do not come from the factory as assembled units; installation of these stairways is more for a journeyman carpenter because the finished four-piece jamb is not furnished and must be built on site. Stringers and treads need assembly, and the door and all hardware have to be installed on site.

I frame the rough opening 2 in. larger than the door opening. This allows me to use 3/4-in. stock for the jamb and still have 1/4 in. of shim space on each side to account for possible framing discrepancies. I rip the jamb stock to a width equal to the joist plus finished ceiling and attic flooring material.

It's possible to attach the finish trim to the jamb while it's still on the floor and then mount the whole unit into the rough opening using braces (called stiff legs or dead men) to hold the jamb to the ceiling while its being shimmed and nailed. But because I work alone, I screw ledgers to the ceiling the same way I do for folding stairs and then apply the trim later.

I nail the hinge side of the jamb to the rough framing and then hang the door with #10, 1-in. pan-head screws. Next I close the door to fine-tune the opening. After eyeballing the crack along the door edge, I move the jamb in and out to produce an even reveal down each side and then shim and nail the jamb.

Next I lay the stringers on sawhorses and thread the ladder rods with washers through the center holes of both stringers so that the stringers will stand on edge. Ladder rods are threaded rods that go under the wood treads, giving strength and support to the sections. I install all but the top three treads into the gains (or dadoes) in the stringers, screw the treads to the stringers, then tighten the nuts on the ladder rods. I always peen the ends of the ladder rods to keep the nuts from falling off. It's important to leave out the top three treads so that I can slide the ladderlike section onto the guide-frame bars at the top of the finished jamb.

When I install the guide frames and the two mounting brackets for the drums that contain the springs, I always predrill all of the holes with a ⁵⁄₆₄-in. bit. After 30 years, you would be amazed to see how the wood pulls away from where the screws were put in without predrilling. This causes a minute split to start, and when I repair sliding stairs that are 30 to 50 years old, the cracks have grown enough that I can stick a finger into them.

Installation of the mounting hardware is pretty straightforward. After putting the stringers onto the guide bars, I attach the cables. Caution: I wear gloves and am careful adjusting the cables' tension around the drums. If the cable slips, I could wind up like *The Old Man and the Sea,* with deep cuts in my hands and no fish dinner.

William T. Cox is a carpenter in Bethel Springs, TN, who specializes in installing and repairing disappearing stairways. He is building an earth shelter.

Sources

American Stairways, Inc.
3807 Lamar Ave.
Memphis, TN 38118
(901) 795-9200

American makes three models of folding disappearing stairways. The smallest has 1x4 treads and stringers and a rough opening of 22 in. by 4 ft. The largest has 1x6 treads, 1x5 stringers, and a rough opening of 2 ft. 6 in. by 5 ft. Scissor hinges join the ladderlike sections. Optional accessories include an R-6 insulated door panel, bright orange rubberized painted treads and a fire-resistant door panel.

Bessler Stairway Co.
3807 Lamar Ave.
Memphis, TN 38118
(901) 795-9200

Bessler is a division of American Stairways, Inc. Bessler makes a folding stairway as well as a sliding stairway that has a one-piece stringer and slides on guide bars counterbalanced by spring-loaded cables.

Bessler's folding stairway has high-quality section hinges that butt when the stairway is opened. Standard features include 1x6 treads and 1x5 stringers, as well as an R-6 insulated door and bright orange rubberized painted treads.

Memphis Folding Stairs
P. O. Box 820305
Memphis, TN 38182
(800) 231-2349

Memphis Folding Stairs makes folding stairs that are very similar to the ones offered by American and Bessler. In fact, a person who worked for Memphis Folding Stairs now owns American Stairways. They also sell an aluminum folding stairway, as well as a heavy-duty wood model with 2x4 rails and 2x6 treads. Memphis sells a thermal airlock for its stairs that covers the stairway opening. It operates like a roll-top desk and has an R-value of 5.

Precision Stair Corp.
5727 Superior Dr.
Morristown, TN 37814
(800) 225-7814

Precision makes metal folding stairways and a fixed aluminum ship ladder with a 63° angle of incline. The company also makes an electrically operated commercial-grade sliding stair that has a switch at both the top and bottom of the stairway.

R. D. Werner Co., Inc.
93 Werner Rd.
Greenville, PA 16125
(724) 588-8600

R. D. Werner is a large ladder manufacturer that also makes the Attic Master, which is its line of folding stairs. Of particular note is its aluminum stairway with adjustable feet and a load capacity of 300 lb. Options include a wood push/pull rod that takes the place of a pull cord, self-adhesive antislip tread tape and a stairway door R-5.71 insulating kit.

Therma-Dome, Inc.
36 Commerce Cir.
Durham, CT 06422
(860) 349-3388

Therma-Dome offers two insulating kits for attic stairs (R-10 and R-13.6) that consist of foil-covered urethane foam boards and touch-fastener tie-downs. These covers seal to the attic floor with a foam gasket. With their high R-values, payback will be quicker in colder climates. The covers cost between $65 and $80. Therma-Dome will fabricate covers for most stairways.

A Staircase of Glass and Maple

■ BY SCOTT McBRIDE

Section through Stair at Stairwell

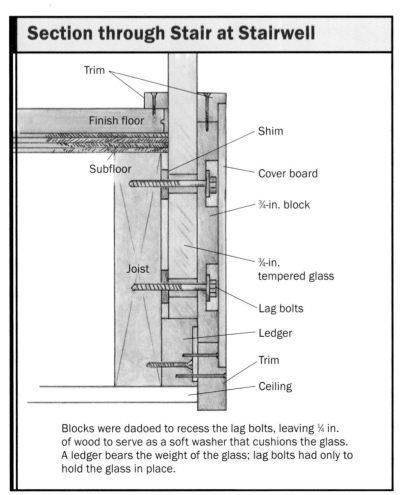

Trim
Finish floor
Shim
Subfloor
Cover board
¾-in. block
Joist
¾-in. tempered glass
Lag bolts
Ledger
Trim
Ceiling

Blocks were dadoed to recess the lag bolts, leaving ¼ in. of wood to serve as a soft washer that cushions the glass. A ledger bears the weight of the glass; lag bolts had only to hold the glass in place.

John Raible practices architecture by trade and builds sculpture by avocation. That spells trouble for the person called upon to render his designs, which often lie somewhere on the borderline between the two disciplines. I built a house recently for one of Raible's clients. The second floor has an open floor plan under a tent-like hip roof. Two staircases, one from the entry foyer and one from the kitchen, lead up to a central stair hall that overlooks the public areas of the first floor. Daylight floods the hall from a number of skylights and cascades into the rooms below. To preserve the dramatic effect of openness and light, Raible called for an open-riser staircase in the foyer. And instead of newels and balusters, the continuous 3-in.-dia. maple handrail was to be supported entirely by ¾-in.-hick panels of tempered glass. Installing the glass was tricky enough, but creating the handrail was even more time-consuming. It called for a number of jigs and lots of patience.

An Invisible Balustrade

The plan was to lag bolt the glass to the stair stringers and to the framing that formed the stairwell, using wood blocks as washers to cushion the glass. Ledgers would bear the weight of the glass, which was considerable, so the bolts would only have to clamp the glass firmly in position.

The glass fabricator needed templates for the glass panels, complete with the location of bolt holes, so I decided to mount these templates in position first, build the handrail on top of them, and then disassemble the whole affair. This would allow me to start work on the handrail almost immediately, and would let me easily reconcile any differences between field conditions and the drawings. The templates were made from ¾-in. plywood, equal to the thickness of the glass, and I reinforced them with 2-in.-wide plywood ribs to ensure that they would stand straight when fastened. This was essential because I had to depend on the top edges of the templates to be an accurate guide for building the handrail.

To prepare the supporting surfaces for glass, I first screwed 1x2 ledgers to the lower edges of the stringers and the stairwell rim joists (see the drawing on p. 146). These ledgers would bear the weight of the glass. Next, I carefully shimmed the mounting surfaces at the location of each bolt. My goal was to align all the bearing points for each

panel in a true vertical plane. This had to be done with precision because any out-of-plumbness over the distance between upper and lower bolts would be amplified at the level of the handrail. Also, if the mounting points were out of alignment it would be easy to twist the glass to the breaking point when tightening the bolts. As it turned out,

Inside- and Outside-Curve Jigs

To form the inside curve of each railing elbow, the author used the sturdy jig shown below. The base of the jig corresponds to the inside diameter of the elbow, and rides against the shaper collar. McBride tightened wingnuts against a caul to secure the workpiece; pointed dog screws added holding power. Slender, removable metal pins were used to shim out the rough stock when the first cuts were made. The pins were removed for subsequent cuts.

After slipping a partially milled elbow into the second jig and snugging up a battery of wingnuts against the caul, the author made another series of cuts to form the outside curve of the elbow. Stout angleiron handles allowed him to keep his hands well away from the cutting action. Conical dog screws helped to keep the elbow in place as it was cut. A stop block registered each elbow in the correct position.

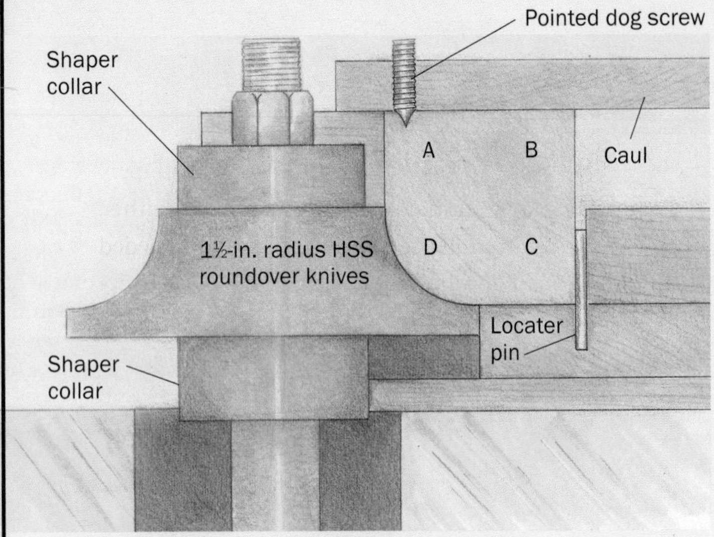

INSIDE-CURVE JIG—FIRST SERIES OF CUTS
This series creates one half of an inside curve. The rough blank is registered against locator pins. The caul clamps the workpiece in place; a pointed dog screw secures it.

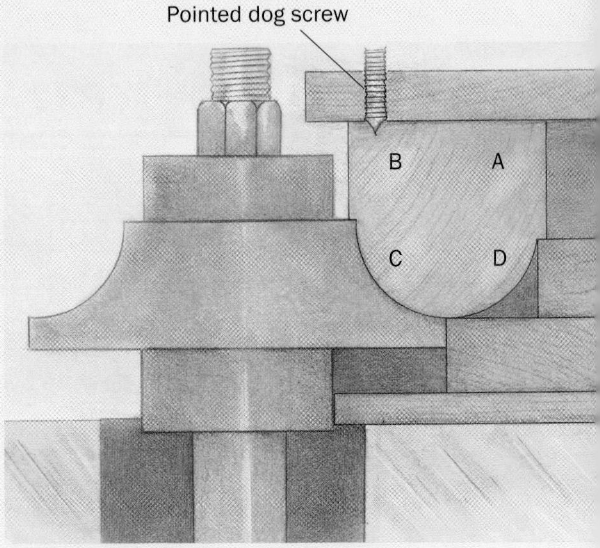

Shaper collar
Pointed dog screw
A B Caul
1½-in. radius HSS roundover knives
D C
Shaper collar
Locater pin

OUTSIDE-CURVE JIG—SECOND SERIES OF CUTS
This series creates one half of an outside curve.

Pointed dog screw
B A
C D

much of this painstaking effort was in vain. The glass panels warped somewhat during the tempering process, which involves baking the glass in a furnace, and this caused plenty of headaches in the final installation.

To keep the glass from cracking, I placed ¾-in. thick vertical blocks between the bolt heads and the glass. The blocks acted as soft

washers, distributing the bolts' pressure over the glass. Each block was dadoed to create a recess for the bolt heads, leaving only ¼ in. of wood between the bolts' metal washer and the glass. The blocks also served as a nail base for the ¼-in. maple plywood cover boards that would conceal this fastening arrangement. Rabbeted horizontal trim pieces were nailed to the tops of the blocks to house the lengthwise edges of the cover boards.

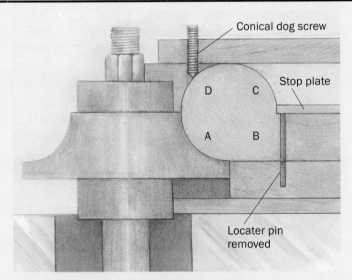

INSIDE-CURVE JIG—THIRD SERIES OF CUTS
This series creates the second half of an inside curve. The outside of the elbow registers against stop plates.

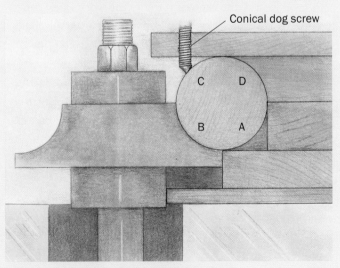

OUTSIDE-CURVE JIG—FINAL SERIES OF CUTS
This creates the second half of an outside curve.

Tooling Up for the Handrail

After bolting all the glass templates into position, I could determine the lengths of handrail I'd need and the number of elbows. Rather than attempt to develop specific falling easements for each change of pitch and direction in the handrail, I made a number of single elbows which, when used singly or in combination with others, would fit any of the conditions found in the two staircases. In principle it would be like making the handrail out of straight lengths of plumbing pipe and various fittings, except for the fact that the wood elbows could be readily cut to any angle between 0° and 90°. As long as these cuts were made through a true radial plane, the resulting section would mate accurately with another elbow or a straight run of rail. The ability to shorten and combine the elbows in this fashion would allow for a fairly graceful flow of the handrail—not so fine as a traditionally lofted handrail, perhaps, but not so crude as a pipe rail either.

To mill the 3-in.-dia. handrail I needed some serious tooling. Although you can scout the catalogs and find a 1½-in. radius roundover bit for a router, the catalog description sometime states that these bits are "not guaranteed." I'm not quite sure what that means, but with so much steel spinning at 22,000 rpm I'd just as soon not find out. A sales representative from Chas. G. G. Schmidt & Co., Inc. fixed me up with a hefty set of ball-bearing shaper collars and a pair of 1½-in. radius roundover knives milled

Straight lengths of handrail were milled on a table saw fitted with a molding cutter. A guide strip mounted to the saw fence engaged a groove in the bottom of the handrail, thereby preventing the handrail from tipping as it moved past the cutter.

Most important, the jigs kept my fingers out of the picture.

from ⅜-in.-thick high-speed steel (HSS). Corrugations on the upper edges of the knives lock them securely between the collars. The sales representative also gave me valuable advice on the design of the jigs I would need to make the elbows safely. "Build them heavy," he warned me, "and keep your hands far away from the cutter." I understood what he meant the first time I set the cutter spinning. It emitted an ominous-sounding "whoosh" and fanned a breeze that gave me a lump in my throat.

Making the Straight Run

Milling the straight runs of rail was simple enough. After dressing solid maple stock to 3 in. by 3 in., I plowed a 1-in.-wide groove on the underside of the stock, using a straight cutter mounted in a table-saw molding cutterhead. This groove would receive the top edge of the glass panels (I allowed a little extra clearance that I could fill later with clear silicone caulk).

With the collar/knife setup mounted on the 1-in.-dia. spindle of my shaper, I made the first, second, and third roundover cuts, with the stock pressed firmly against the table and fence by a hold-down. To prevent the work from rolling as I completed the last roundover cut, I mounted a 1-in.-wide guide strip to the outboard side of the fence (see the photo above). This strip engaged the glass groove as the finished rail exited past the cutter.

Building the Elbow Jigs

Making the elbows proved to be much more complex than making the straight lengths of handrail. To shape the elbows I needed two jigs: one to form the outside curve and one to shape the inside curve (see the photos on p. 148). The jigs securely held each curved elbow blank in place for successive passes over the shaper knife. Most important, the jigs kept my fingers out of the picture.

Both jigs are similar in construction. A base rides against the lower ball-bearing shaper collar to guide the cuts. I veneered the underside of each base with plastic laminate to allow it to glide freely on the shaper table. The front edge corresponds to the inside or outside curve of the elbow, and determines the shape of the cut. Because the minor diameter of the cutter was offset by ¼ in. from the collar, the template curve and the cutting curve had to be slightly different. The purpose of the ¼-in. offset was to provide clearance so that the slightly oversize blank would not rub against the upper collar during the first two series of passes.

Attached to each jig base is a layer of 5/4 poplar lumber. This layer lifts the workpiece so that the outermost portion of the shaper knife can reach under the work when cutting. This layer also holds captive the countersunk heads of carriage bolts; wingnuts and washers on the ends of the bolts put pressure on a caul that grips the workpiece securely.

Other elements of the jig's anatomy included a fence against which the workpiece would rest, stop blocks for registering the ends of the blanks, and a pair of stout angle-iron handles for the outside-curve jig (the other jig could be used safely without handles). T-nuts embedded in the cauls held dog screws that helped to secure each workpiece. I filed sharp points on two of the dog screws used for the inside curve jig, figuring that this would give them extra purchase on the first two passes on the rough blank. Dog screws with a gentler 45° conical point were used on the third and fourth passes; they were positioned to exert a firm downward and inward pressure on the elbow's finished surfaces.

To form each elbow, I'd have to make four series of passes: two for the inside curve and two for the outside curve (see the drawings on pp. 148-149). Each series would form either an upper or a lower half of the elbow. In each series of passes the knife was raised in ⅛-in. increments for successive passes until the full 1½-in. depth of cut was reached. Cutting a little at a time reduced the load on the shaper and produced a better finish in the final pass. Tearout, which would have been a real problem with softer wood, was minimal with the close-grained maple, even on the short-grain sections of the curve.

The Inside Curve

I began by thicknessing wide maple stock to 3 in. and bandsawing the blanks to rough shape, leaving an extra ⅛ in. on the inside and outside curves. The first series of passes would be made with the elbow locked into the inside-curve jig. For the initial cuts, I wouldn't have a true surface to work from, only the rough edges of the bandsawn blank. I'd need at least ⅛ in. of clearance between the fence and the elbow to accommodate the extra stock, and probably a bit more in places, so I made the fence to the elbow's

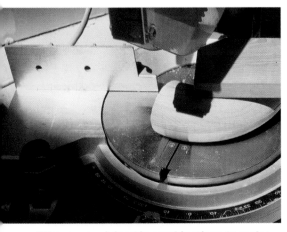

Elbows were joined in combinations to make handrail easements, so the cuts between elbows had to be precise. To secure the elbows to his miter-saw table, the author drilled the table for a threaded stud and used it to secure a clamp block.

outside radius of 5 in. and added ¼ in. to that. This offset provided clearance for the oversize blank as did the previously described offset between cutter and collar.

To position the blank approximately in the inside curve jig for the first passes, I installed a pair of removable ⅛-in.-dia. pins against the curve of the fence, and snugged the blank against the pins (see the drawings on pp. 148-149).

The Rest of the Curve

After I cut the first half of the inside curve, the freshly milled surface could be registered against the convex fence of the outside-curve jig for the next series of cuts. The fence on this jig had been sized to the elbow's exact inside radius of 2 in. because the fence would be registering only previously milled surfaces. After locking the elbow into place, I made the second series of cuts, forming the lower outside curve of the elbow.

For the third series of cuts, I switched the elbow back to the inside-curve jig. Now I needed to reduce the radius of the inside-curve fence so it would register properly against the trued outside edge just cut in the second series. To do this, I slipped a pair of curved, ¼-in. plywood stop plates into the jig, just above the fence. The inside edges of each plate would ride against the outer circumference of the elbow, just above the midpoint of its thickness (see the top drawing on p. 149). That way the plates wouldn't interfere with the as yet unmilled portion of the blank. For the fourth and final series of passes, it was back to the outside-curve jig. This series of passes corresponded to those made in the second series of passes.

Making Accurate Radial Cuts

A 15-in. power miter box (Hitachi® #C15FB) was used to cut the elbows and the handrails to length. Positioning the elbows for accurate radial cutting, though, took some thought.

To drill clearance holes for handrail bolts, the author used another jig. The drill bit was guided by a center hold drilled in a guide block of oak.

Assembling the Handrail

To join the handrails to the elbows, I used double-ended handrail bolts, which have a machine thread on one end and a lag thread on the other. To connect elbows to each other, I used dowel screws; they have a lag thread on both ends.

To drill accurate pilot holes in the elbows and the railing, I built drilling jigs. These were just squared-up blocks of oak, drilled on a drill press and fastened to one of two bases. One base supported straight lengths of rail that were secured by a pipe vise (see the photo at left). The other was for elbows, using a rod-and-nut clamping arrangement similar to the one used earlier for the miter box. The clearance hole in the handrail was drilled oversize to provide some margin for error in aligning the elbow to the handrail. A nut pocket mortised into the underside of the handrails intercepted the clearance hole, giving me just enough room to slip a nut onto the machine screw and tighten it with a box wrench.

The handrail bolts made a rock-solid joint as far as keeping the parts from sepa- rating, but I was worried about misalign- ment of the joints over the years. To ensure that this would not occur, I keyed the parts together after assembly using a plate joiner. Biscuits were let halfway into the handrail surface in inconspicuous locations. After the glue dried, the biscuits were shaved down flush and the joints were faired with planes, rasps, and sandpaper. Finally, the gap be- tween the glass and the outside edges of the glass groove was filled with silicone caulk, forming a bond between the glass and the handrail.

Scott McBride is a frequent contributor to Fine Homebuilding *magazine and the author of* Build Like a Pro: Windows and Doors *and* Landscaping with Wood, *both by The Taunton Press, Inc. His mill- work business is located in Sperryville, VA.*

The Hitachi has a replaceable table insert with a slot the exact width of the blade kerf. I drew a pencil line on the table, running it across the faces of the split fence, and it crossed the slot at the imaginary center point. Measuring 5 in. out from this point along the left fence (the radius of the outside curve of an elbow), I drew a vertical line on the fence. By positioning the outside circumference of an elbow against the line while butting its end tight to the fence, I would ensure a radial cut. Because the pivot point of the miter box lies behind the fence, however, the center point would shift slightly from left to right when cutting different angles. I adjusted the vertical line on the fence for the different cuts, in each case measuring 5 inches from wherever the plane of the fence crossed the cutting slot.

To hold the elbows securely while cutting them, I drilled the miter-box table for a threaded stud. A clamp block and nut atop the stud left my hands clear of the action (see the photo on p. 151). With a 100-tooth carbide blade on the saw, the result was a cut smooth as glass.

CREDITS

p. ii: Photo by Scott Phillips, © The Taunton Press, Inc.

p. iii: Photo by Scott Phillips, © The Taunton Press, Inc.

p. iv: (left) Photo © Sharon Mills; (right) Photo by Roe A. Osborn, courtesy of *Fine Homebuilding,* © The Taunton Press, Inc. p. v: (left) Photo © Stephen Winchester; (center) Photo by Roe A. Osborn, courtesy of *Fine Homebuilding,* © The Taunton Press, Inc.; (right) Photo © Glen Stewart

p. 4: Cutting Out Basic Stairs by Eric Pfaff, issue 100. Photos by Roe A. Osborn, courtesy of *Fine Homebuilding,* © The Taunton Press, Inc.; Illustrations by © Christopher Clapp.

p. 11: A Site-Built Stair by Alexander Brennen, issue 62. Photo by Charles Miller, courtesy of *Fine Homebuilding,* © The Taunton Press, Inc.; Illustrations by Michael Mandarano, © The Taunton Press, Inc.

p. 17: Using a Story Pole to Lay Out Stairs by Lon Schleining, issue 142. Photos by Charles Bickford, courtesy of *Fine Homebuilding,* © The Taunton Press, Inc.; Illustration by Dan Thornton, © The Taunton Press, Inc.

p. 20: Building an L-Shaped Stair by Larry Haun, issue 67. Photos © Roger Turk/Northlight Photography; Illustrations by Bob Goodfellow, © The Taunton Press, Inc.

p. 26: A Veteran Stairbuilder's Tools and Tips by Michael von Deckbar-Frabbiele, issue 92. Illustrations by Bob Goodfellow, © The Taunton Press, Inc.

p. 33: A Quick Way to Build a Squeak-Free Stair by Alan Ferguson, issue 104. Photos © Sharon Mills; Illustration © Kathleen Rushton.

p. 45: Hanging a Wall Railing by Sebastian Eggert, issue 125. Photos by Roe A. Osborn, courtesy of *Fine Homebuilding,* © The Taunton Press, Inc.; Illustration by Dan Thornton, © The Taunton Press, Inc.

p. 52: Building a Custom Box Newel by Lon Schleining, issue 134. Photos by Charles Bickford, courtesy of *Fine Homebuilding,* © The Taunton Press, Inc.

p. 60: Building Finish Stairs by Andy Engel, issue 114. (pp. 60, 70) Photos by Andy Engel, courtesy of *Fine Homebuilding,* © The Taunton Press, Inc.; (pp. 63-64, 67-69) Photos by Scott Phillips, © The Taunton Press, Inc.; (pp. 61, 65, 66) Photos © Patricia Steed; Illustration by Chuck Lockhart, © The Taunton Press, Inc.

p. 71: Building an Exterior Newel Post by Peter Carlson, issue 84. Photos by Chuck Miller, courtesy of *Fine Homebuilding,* © The Taunton Press, Inc., except p. 72 Photo © Peter Carlson; Illustrations by Bob Goodfellow, © The Taunton Press, Inc.

p. 78: Installing Stair Skirtboards by Bob Syvanen, issue 68. Illustrations by Bob Goodfellow, © The Taunton Press, Inc.

p. 82: Making a Bullnose Starting Step by Stephen Winchester, issue 82. Photos © Stephen Winchester, except p. 83 Photo by Rich Ziegner, courtesy of *Fine Homebuilding,* © The Taunton Press, Inc.; Illustrations by Bob Goodfellow, © The Taunton Press, Inc.

p. 92: Making a Curved Handrail by John Griffin, issue 129. Photos by Andy Engel, courtesy of *Fine Homebuilding,* © The Taunton Press, Inc., except p. 93 (full-page) Photo © Ron Ruscio; Illustration by Dan Thornton, © The Taunton Press, Inc.

p. 102: A Balustrade of Branches by Dan Davis, issue 130. Photos © Zachary Zdinak, except p. 105 (left) Photo © Dennis Thomann

p. 106: A Freestanding Spiral Stair by Stephen M. White, issue 110. Photos by Charles Miller, courtesy of *Fine Homebuilding,* © The Taunton Press, Inc.; Illustrations by Bob Goodfellow, © The Taunton Press, Inc.

p. 118: Capping a Curved Stair Wall by John Griffin, issue 118. Photos © John Griffin, except p. 188 Photo by Andy Engel, courtesy of *Fine Homebuilding,* © The Taunton Press, Inc.; Illustrations © Paul Perreault

p. 123: Framing curved Stairs on Site by Scott Paschal, issue 110. Photos © Scott Paschal, except p. 123 Photo © Ron Ruscio; Illustrations by Dan Thornton, © The Taunton Press, Inc.

p. 128: Cantilevered Stairway by Rob Harlan, issue 91. Photos © John Birchard

p. 132: A Stair in the Air by Glen Stewart, issue 140. Photos © Glen Stewart, except p. 132 Photo by Roe A. Osborn, courtesy of *Fine Homebuilding,* © The Taunton Press, Inc., and p. 138 (left) Photo © Kris Stewart; Illustrations by Dan Thornton, © The Taunton Press, Inc.

p. 139: Disappearing Attic Stairways by William T. Cox, issue 89. Photos by Jefferson Kolle, courtesy of *Fine Homebuilding,* © The Taunton Press, Inc., except p. 142 (right) Photo © William T. Cox

p. 146: A Staircase of Glass and Maple by Scott McBride, issue 60. Photos by Scott McBride, courtesy of *Fine Homebuilding,* © The Taunton Press, Inc., except pp. 147-148 Photos by Mark Freier, courtesy of *Fine Homebuilding,* © The Taunton Press, Inc.; Illustrations by Michael Mandarano, © The Taunton Press, Inc.

INDEX

Index note: page references in *italics* indicate a photograph; references in **bold** indicate a drawing. Page references in ***bold and italics*** indicate a drawing and photograph on the page.